Family Reunion

Family Reunion:
Poems about Parenting Grown Children

Edited by

Sondra Zeidenstein

Chicory Blue Press, Inc.
Goshen, Connecticut 06756

Chicory Blue Press, Inc.
Goshen, Connecticut 06756
www.chicorybluepress.com
© 2003 by Sondra Zeidenstein. All rights reserved.
Printed in the United States of America.

Cover photograph © 2003 by George Zeidenstein
Book Designer: Virginia Anstett
Additional acknowledgments appear on pages 105-107

Library of Congress Cataloging-in-Publication Data

Family reunion : poems about parenting grown children / edited by
Sondra Zeidenstein
    p.   cm.
  ISBN 1-887344-07-1 (pbk.)
  1. Parent and adult child – Poetry. 2. Parenting – Poetry.
  3. Family – Poetry. 4. American poetry. I. Zeidenstein, Sondra.

PS595.P37 F36 2003
811.008'0355 – dc21

                              2002034900

This book is dedicated to my beloved sister, Jan Feldman,
who couldn't wait to see it.

Acknowledgments

I am grateful to many, many poets and friends and relatives for enthusiastic support of this anthology. I am particularly grateful to Jill Breckenridge, Betty Buchsbaum, Cortney Davis, Geraldine Zetzel and George Zeidenstein for their constructive criticism of the introduction. I thank the Ragdale Foundation and its gracious staff for providing me time and space to hear myself thinking.

Notes toward a Conversation
in Poetry

I.

I've just spent a week as part of a poetry workshop where participants
and teachers alike are expected to write and read to each other seven
poems in seven days. Five great poets presided, sixty-one good poets
participated, the vast majority under forty-five; I was the oldest partici-
pant by at least six years. Pressures to produce were extreme. Every-
one was ambitious for acceptance and praise – and very anxious. I'd
been there five times before, had my share of success and my share of
hard days. This was the hardest. This time I'd *arrived* in bad shape.

The very day before departure, my grown daughter had left a
message in a strained voice on our answering machine, saying some-
thing that hurt me like an unexpected slap. *We'll have to talk about it*,
she concluded, *but not now.* There was no possibility of getting back to
her before I left. I was furious, ranting to my husband, and, at the
underside of my rage, feeling a paralyzing despair. No other thoughts
or emotions could take hold in my mind – not on the plane, at the
baggage claim, in the Reno hotel, on the long ride up along the Truc-
kee River, at orientation, in bed that first night, all week long. Noth-
ing soothed me. I couldn't sleep. I cried in the night. I cried in the
middle of every poem I wrote. Color bled from the landscape. I gave
up any hope for ease and happiness in the years remaining to me.

Of course some part of me – teeny, barely audible – knew this
pain wasn't born of tragedy like death or terrible illness. But I could
not write about anything else. Here I was, jet-lagging at 6500 feet,
among poets – many the age of my daughter, many writing about *their*
mothers – who had never read a poem about what I was experienc-
ing, because no-one had written it. My poem a day would come from
this rawness or from nowhere.

Struggling to write out of this particular kind of pain, I was acutely
aware that I had almost no mentors. In the last thirty years, literature
has transformed African-American experience, gay and lesbian expe-
rience, most aspects of women's experience, including, through

hundreds and hundreds of poems, as if in conversation with each other, our complicated relationships with our mothers and fathers. But rarely have I found this segment of human experience, the parenting of grown children, in poems. It simply wasn't part of the continuum.

In six days, I wrote myself from paralysis to pain to anger, then to a centered, balanced place from which I haven't since been thrown very far. But I have never been so humbled as a poet, so humiliated. Only a handful of participants responded to my poems. Almost no-one said the poems were good. They *weren't* good. How could they have been? I was too raw, the territory too new and frightening, too unimagined. How could I take it and myself seriously?

Here is the poem I eventually pieced together from the week's outpouring. It expresses, I think, the point from which I could begin to move to anger and reconciliation:

Separating

> I don't want to be up in the middle of the night,
> mourning the loss of my daughter
> as she separates from me.
> *Separates.*
> Word that reminds me of yolk and albumen,
> that sounds like nothing much
> except my daughter is 46, I'm 69
> and lie awake for hours sorrowing.
> My daughter says she's putting her own family first now.
> (Fine.)
> No more free pass into her life.
> (Poor Mom.)
> Reader, how can I draw you to me
> when this is not death, not illness
> but my daughter, whose weighty curls
> I long to weave my fingers through.
> I need her. We laid paths for each other
> in the tangled neurons of our brains,

she lives in me, intuition quick as mine –

                                    my daughter

feels trapped, hacks her way out.
Can you understand what it's like to be me,
my daughter packing up, speckles in her irises
retrieved, eloquent eyebrows?
You were secretive, she blames.
I know. She needs to do this,
will be the better for it.

                             But the earth turns pocked,

gouges and cracks. Nothing ripens.
I am a wasp sucked dry.

                        I am forsaken.

There. I've said *something*.
I'm crying writing it.
I start there, kissing my own shoulder.

II.

The other night I watched *First Person Plural*, a PBS documentary that illustrates something I've been thinking about a lot: how little I know, as a parent, about my children's inner life even as they were growing up under my watchful eye.

The filmmaker, Deann Borshay Liem, was born in South Korea to a family reduced to poverty by war. When her widowed mother couldn't afford to keep her, Deann was placed in an orphanage. When she was nine, she was adopted by a well-off American family who were told she was an orphan. Family pictures show Deann's bewildered sadness change to smiles and pleasure in all things American, show her mother and father enchanted by her. By the time she is in high school, everything about her is as stereotypically American as being a cheerleader. In fact, she is a cheerleader, almost indistinguishable from her perky all-American sister. She has no accent, doesn't remember a word of Korean, never speaks of her years in the orphanage, of anything about Korea.

After college, however, she begins to experience flashes of memory, that come with no warning, of the orphanage and of other scenes from her life in Korea. When she writes to the orphanage to see if she can track down her dead family, she is told she isn't an orphan, that she had been sent to America to replace a real orphan who had gotten sick at the last minute.

The documentary records how Deann locates her family in Korea, visits them, tells her American parents the whole story, takes them to visit her Korean family to whom she speaks through an interpreter. Deann films the hugs and tears of her Korean mother, the hugs and tears of her American mother and father who find it hard to accept that her biological mother has any claim on *their* daughter's life or emotions. Even her Korean mother tells her to accept the American mother as her own.

The filmmaker tells how deeply at home she feels in Korea, surrounded by people with hair like hers, her coloring, her eyes. She films herself telling her American mother and father that all the time she was being raised in America, she was feeling, deep in her consciousness, that if she behaved well enough, if she passed "the test," she would get back to her home in Korea. The American family cannot believe that this division had existed behind the smiling eyes of their perfect daughter. Why didn't you realize I needed to grieve for what I had lost, she questions. Why didn't you ever ask me, why didn't you try to get me to tell you how I felt? It seemed to me you didn't care for me, for who I really was. You didn't want to know.

The mother replies, I don't know why I didn't ask you. Then she pauses, wounded, but not angry or defensive. I guess I was afraid to find out that you felt some separation from us. The father, though clearly loving, is defensive: If you had said any of this when you were younger, the way you're saying it now, we could have talked, let it all out, looked at it. But you didn't.

Neither of them acknowledges what we, the audience, seeing the whole sorrowful story, feel – that the parents *should* have been able to ask and to listen. *Someone* should have been. The daughter has a look on her face, subtle, but real and unrehearsed, that says she hasn't been fully understood or acknowledged. And that she won't be. Everyone has good intentions, but the daughter's experience is given its due, validated, only by the documentary.

For me, the documentary goes well beyond the divided mind of a child adopted from a foreign country. It illustrates a universal disjunction: that parents don't know the world their child experienced growing up. Parents often do not acknowledge, even to themselves, that it might be different from what they remember. It is the child who has to recover and verify that world on her own. Often parents find it uncomfortable to hear their child's version. I imagine my adult daughter, for example, poring over the poems I published about my secret love affairs during her childhood as if they were validating texts. For her, they were. Only now do I understand how my secretiveness deceived *her*, though I never intended her harm. I have just seen Liv Ullman's movie *Faithless* and am astonished by her relentless exploration of how desire and adultery explode the nuclear family, causing aftershocks of pain, treachery, even death. Everything spoiled. As I am stunned by reading what the Dalai Lama says about inappropriate sensual desire: *it is like licking honey from the cutting edge of a sword*. I never imagined! I only thought of the honey.

I find it acutely painful to acknowledge that my child experienced as harmful my attempt to raise her lovingly and protect her from harm. I don't want to accept it. I want this child to have benefited from the good intentions of her parents. I want her to have been transformed by the love her parents genuinely felt. I don't want her to have absorbed and been wounded by her parents' fears and inadequacies and strategies for survival. But I take responsibility. I work hard, as mother of an adult child, to hold in my consciousness the double vision: how I experienced loving my child vs. how she experienced being "loved." This is old news to therapists, that the adult child continues to carry the long-ago parent, still mythically powerful, inside her, even when the present parent is expanding and changing, *going on being*. But how long it's taken for me to know it, to accept it as inevitable.

Only now that I'm old, and my children middle-aged, can I imagine how my behavior was experienced by my young children. I needed time, the perspective of years – of age – to look at my behavior, to own it, reinterpret it in the light of long experience. I needed to accept myself and to see that I am no different than anyone else. I needed to get over shame, defensiveness, guilt: If only I'd spent more time holding them, comforting them. If only I'd known how to confront my spouse with my grievances instead of acting out my anger. If I'd stood up for the children when he yelled at them. If I'd guided them more strenuously. If I'd not been so constantly at the edge of my own pain that I couldn't tolerate *their* pain or allow them to express it. If only I hadn't been so needy that I merged with them to feel whole. If I'd fed them from my breasts. If I'd held them in the middle of the night when they cried. If I hadn't been depressed....

Recently I heard Lucille Clifton read a short poem that touched on this burden of guilt many parents carry, in a way I hadn't come across before. The poem is about a newborn German baby and its loving German mother, cooing and fussing, coaxing a smile, confident she will raise this baby well. She wonders what she should name such a beautiful infant. *Gunther?* No. *Heinrich?* No. And then the poem ends: *Adolf?* Yes, *Adolf.* We never know how a baby, a child, is going to turn out, Clifton said later, talking about the poem that had so disturbed its listeners. I'd only heard that shocking (to me) statement once before, from a poet friend who, because she has the experience of mental illness in her family, worries at the birth of each new grandchild. What a new thought for those of us who've spent our child-raising years feeling responsible for anything and everything that our children would become. In fact, being *told* we are responsible by all the books, the doctors, the authorities who governed our earnestness. *We never know how a child is going to turn out.* What a relief that is! What a crap shoot! Why, then, do we still find it so hard to give up feeling responsible?

III.

There is not much poetry about parenting grown children. A significant vacuum, considering how much they are part of the experience of so many of us who are older. I am 69. My children are 46 and 45, my grandsons 21 and 11. I am a poet, a student of poetry, an avid reader. Literature, poetry especially, has always taught me more about myself than I know from my own particular experience. Why shouldn't I expect to find poems that express the extraordinary sorrow and rage I felt when my daughter was finally determined to separate from me? Who is making images and music of this experience? Are there so few poets, particularly women, with adult children? Are so few of us moved to write about these relationships, these emotions? I look to poems for evidence that I'm not the only one floundering. Or that I am the only one. If that's the case, I need to know that too.

As I began to look deliberately for writing about being parents of grown children, I remembered Raymond Carver's poems about his son's and daughter's drinking problems. I was amazed that Carver had written about his children from some other stance than perfect devotion and wondrous love. I thought of Hayden Carruth's "Pittsburgh," set in the hospital where his daughter is being treated for liver cancer. I recalled a poem by Sheila Gardiner, "Five for Lunch," in which she writes: *I think suddenly of my son, a middle-aged stranger,/ of my daughters who can barely keep their own sorrows/ at rapier's end....* I remembered a poet's response to the rape of her grown daughter. I remembered a great poet's poem I heard at a workshop, calling on the full moon to watch over her son who was living on the streets.

I thought of relevant work in prose, though rarely in non-fiction. Recent exceptions are Joanna Macy's memoir, *Widening Circles*, and Maxine Kumin's account of her recovery from a broken neck, *Inside the Halo and Beyond*, which include unusually honest tributes to grown children. Most heart-expanding for me is a column by Patricia Smith in *Ms*. She writes about a phone call from her son in prison. *Most of the time I just let the phone ring. If I pick up the receiver, this is the way it goes. There's that blip of echo air and I say, "Hello? Hello?" before his new mama, disembodied white female middle-American all-purpose monotone, informs me that I have a collect call from an inmate of the Middlesex House of Corrections. And in that space of silence left open for his name, my son barks, "Damon," deep, guttural, and badass, and Oh, I think, blindwalking into what now passes for normal conversation, it's just my son phoning from bondage to say good-night. And to tell me that some guy in his cell plans to murder him in his sleep.* No personal essay I've ever read touched on that kind of experience.

I was reassured by the number of contemporary novels and stories that focus on relationships with grown children. Rosellen Brown's *Before and After* is written from the points of view of parents who face the possibility that their grown son has murdered his girlfriend. It is about the parents' responses – the mother's different from the father's – to a grown child's unthinkable behavior. (Nadine Gordimer's *The House Gun*, the movie *The Deep End* are variations of that plot.) The sad novel, *The Disgrace*, by J.M. Coetzee, includes lessons a father learns from his adult daughter's extreme and yet realistic choices about how to live her life in politically and historically compromised South Africa. Doris Lessing's always contemporary *Golden Notebooks*, written forty plus years ago, contains long sections in which a mother, concerned by her grown son's depression, shares her worries in compassionate conversations with her best friend. In Philip Roth's *I Married a Communist*, I found for the first time a portrayal of an enmeshed mother and grown daughter that incisively revealed how destructive such symbiosis can be for both women. I'd lived in proximity to such a relationship all my life, hurtful, festering, unnamed, but had never seen it so openly given language and dimension, humanized. I thought of Tema Nason's story, "Full Moon," about the hospital visit a mother makes to her mentally ill adult daughter. For the first time, the mother, from whose point of view this story is told, sees that the demands of the adult daughter's illness are perpetual, and allows herself, if only for a moment, to feel her own need: *But what about me?*

When I interviewed Tema Nason, who is, also, author of *Ethel: A Fictional Autobiography of Ethel Rosenberg*, and a feminist, a risk-taker in all her writing, about her writing life, she made comments that have been seeds for this anthology. She felt that our generation of older women writers who've parented children steers clear of that subject matter in our work: we don't write about what it is like to be mothers. *I don't think there are many women of my generation born in the twenties or early thirties writing their stories. And our stories must not be lost. The role of the mother is so sanctified in our society and yet demeaned in another way. You're so easily at fault. You're either a saint or a sinner. For a writer to honestly talk about the ambivalent feelings–the frustration, anger, the hostility that comes up at times, all the negative feelings that I think women are afraid of tackling – as well as the abiding love and deep attachment and concern – all this, it's loaded and a cultural taboo. And I believe it is a subject that has to be tackled. Otherwise we'll never know the mother's voice.* I think the same thing can be said about the father's voice, which is bound to be different. I long to hear it.

It is Toni Morrison who, as usual, goes farther in her imaginative reach than any of us. Through the character Eva in her novel, *Sula*, she takes the relationship between mother and adult child to its extreme. Eva, whose husband walked out on her when their children were small, leaving her with "nothing but three beets," raised the children alone, through every hazard and disaster. At one point, she had to abandon them, staying away for eight years, and returning minus a leg but with enough money to build a boarding house. Now her son, Plum, has come home from the war, a heroin addict, hanging around the house with a weak grin, sleeping in a room she gives him downstairs, while she lives mostly in seclusion on the third floor. One day Eva comes down to Plum's room, sits by his bed watching him in his drugged doze, shocked when she picks up what she thinks is a glass of strawberry soda and sees it is watery blood. Gradually she pulls the semi-conscious man toward her from the bed, holds him close to her body in motherly intimacy, rocking and lulling him. Then she goes out to the kitchen, brings back a container of liquid, pours it over him, throws a match on him, walks out and closes the door. Morrison gives Eva a long compelling speech to explain her murder of her son. In short, she says it was because he wouldn't grow up, he was never going to become a man: *There wasn't space for him in my womb. And he was crawlin' back....I birthed him once. I couldn't do it again. He was growed, a big old thing. Godhavemercy, I couldn't birth him twice....I done everything I could to make him leave me and go on and live and be a man but he wouldn't and I had to keep him out so I just thought of a way he could die like a man not all scrunched up inside my womb, but like a man.*

Well!

IV.

What *is* the nature of our relationship to our grown children? Is it biologically vestigial, like the appendix or adenoids, liable to infection and rupture, otherwise of little use? Are we hangnails to them for the rest of our lives? Or ulcers? I have puzzled for years over my maternal feelings for my grown children, amazed at the passion I feel when I am with them, unable to separate who they are, from who they were, from who I am. When I leave them, it takes me hours, even days to get back to my own separate self again.

Once it was necessary for my love to be this powerful. I had to be, and was, willing with no forethought to throw my life under a bus or into deep water or fire to save my boy and girl. I watched over them anxiously, as if something bad was bound to happen if I didn't. Such passion has the force of an opened hydrant. But there is no fire. It is superfluous, inappropriate. My children don't need or want it. I fight it, try to wrestle it down, this unrequited passion beyond any I've known.

In her book, *Woman: An Intimate Geography*, Natalie Angier writes the only words I've read or heard anywhere that can begin to explain the quality of love I feel in the presence of my grown children. *Years and years after a woman has delivered a child, she continues to carry vestiges of that child in her body. I'm talking about tangible vestiges now, not memories. Stray cells from a growing fetus circulate through a woman's body during pregnancy, possibly as a way for the fetus to communicate with the mother's immune system and forestall its ejection from the body as the foreign object it is. The fetal-maternal cell dialogue was thought to be a short-lived one, lasting only as long as the pregnancy. Recently, though, scientists have found fetal cells surviving in the maternal bloodstream decades after the women have given birth to their children. The cells didn't die; they didn't get washed away. They persisted, and may have divided a few times in the interim. They're fetal cells, which means they've got a lot of life built into them. A mother, then, is forever a cellular chimera, a blend of the body she was born with and of all the bodies she has borne. Which may mean nothing, or it may mean that there is always something there to remind her, a few biochemical bars of a song capable of playing upon her neural systems of attachment, particularly if those attachments were nourished through a multiplicity of stimuli, of sensorial input – the hormonal pageantry of gestation, the odors of fetal urine, the great upheaval of delivery, and the sight and touch of the newborn. This* makes sense of my feelings.

As does the writing of three California psychiatrists, Thomas Lewis, Fari Amini and Richard Lannon, in *The General Theory of Love*, which explores the relationship of our three-part human brain to our emotional well-being. Of the three parts, reptilian, limbic and neo-cortical, they point out, it is the limbic brain all mammals share that is responsible for the emotional bond that develops between mother and infant and ensures that the baby will be protected and will develop. (I like to assume that this process also involves nurturing fathers.) It's as if a specific, permanent pathway between parent and child is laid down among their millions of tangled neurons. *Limbic resonance* is the name they give this process. It is the right name for what I continue to feel toward my grown children. But when that attachment is broken, not only by death, but by the necessary departure of our grown children? *Given the open-loop physiology of mammals and their dependence on limbic regulation, attachment interruptions are dangerous....like a shattered knee or a scratched cornea, relationship ruptures deliver agony. Most people say that no pain is greater than losing someone they love.* This is certainly the stuff of poems.

V.

Maybe because of the absence of poems about parenting grown children, there seems to be little unguarded "real-life" conversation about these relationships. In her poem "Children," Carolyn Kizer writes of an unspoken pact she has with her friends: *Don't ask me about my children, and I won't inquire of yours.* Reading that was a relief. I am always uncomfortable about how to respond to the inevitable question, when good friends meet: *and how are the children?* My mother reported about her grown children only the things that brought her credit in her status-conscious community: what our husbands did, how many children we had, the kinds of houses we owned, etc. After my older sister had a breakdown, my mother stopped seeing friends. How could she talk about what was really going on? What else was there left to talk about? She couldn't do what Lucy did – Lucy who worked as laundress for my mother and her friends for thirty years, who lived in a segregated community, whose last name I never knew. Only at Lucy's funeral did we learn that the twin daughters she'd always "boasted" about, whose growing up paralleled ours, didn't exist at all. Lucy didn't have twins. She had only one daughter, who was retarded.

I am not so different from my mother and Lucy. When my son was living on a small boat with no phone for several years, sending a postcard every three months or so, it was almost impossible for me to tell that to anyone. Since I could no longer put my son's life in a packaged story, the one about wife, family, profession, hobby, that I felt made *me* acceptable, I didn't want to talk about family any more.

I look around at the grown children of my friends today. Most of them are living, like mine, textured, layered, hard-to-manage lives. Some of them are not succeeding in their work lives or are having problems with weight or addiction, are perfectionists or liars, are excessively permissive with their children, or hire nannies to be, are bullies, have got the wrong politics or religions, are getting divorced, or falling sick. Yet telling the truth about our concerns and experiences as their parents is so rare as to be shocking. When a friend says her husband of thirty years walked out on her, I ask, "How do you feel?" When someone tells me she has cancer, I ask "What did the doctor say?" And then we talk and talk. But when a friend tells me her daughter forbade her to visit her grandchildren, I don't know what to say next. I am afraid to know more. When the fine poet Ruth Whitman published a prose piece in *Sojourner* a dozen years ago, saying that her daughters had cut her off from all contact with them and her grandchildren, I felt more of the jolt of a taboo being broached in her writing than when I read about Kathryn Harrison's love affair with her father in *The Kiss*.

In the last forty years there has been much more poetry about mothering and fathering *young* children than there used to be. Though much of it was written after my own children were grown, I celebrate every inch of this new territory. Such writing has helped me, in retrospect, to understand my experience, to reassess and expand my limited views. I think of birthing poems by Toi Derricotte and Sharon Olds, child-raising poems by Alicia Ostriker, Peter Meinke, Galway Kinnell, Li Young Lee, Brenda Hillman, Len Roberts, poems of a child's pubescence and adolescence by Sue Ellen Thompson, Wendy Mnookin and, of course, Anne Sexton – to mention a few of very many.

But I am of the generation of poets with grown children. The generations after me, so much bolder already than many of us who came of age in the 1940's and 50's, will be older than I am now before their late-born children are adult. I'll be gone. *Now* is the time to extend the poetic imagination to this aspect of our experience. What is holding us back? In a workshop a few years ago, a poet read a poem about her response to her grown daughter's anger, whose chilling first lines, addressing the reader, said something like: *don't ever say a word about this poem to anyone, don't whisper about it, even to me, I never wrote it, you never heard it.* Then what is permissible for us to write?

VI.

It's July, more than a year since I started the preceding pages. In that time, I've gathered sixty-five poems for this anthology I wanted to create. Ready now to assemble the book, I've taken a break for the last few days, because my grown son and *his* grown son have come to visit. We sit on the screened-in porch much of the time, our easy, rambling talk almost drowned out by songbirds and the whirring of hummingbirds at our feeders. With my husband, I prepare light summer meals, fresh lettuce leaves from the garden, small assertive radishes, thick scallions, salads slick with crumbled feta. I lose all touch with my other life – my desire to swim in the summer pond or cut through weeds in the vegetable garden, not to speak of writing poems and working on this anthology.

My son at 46: I immerse myself in his presence. It is hard to pay attention to conversation, though he is thoughtful, full of knowledge, practical, interesting. My fingers want to draw his well-proportioned face, his precise hairline, with a few bold lines, as Picasso drew his. This love, I think, is like the cup of milky chai I'm drinking, with spices that raise my body temperature. I'm grateful to be near him for four days, and then to have him go away, back to his complex life, the details of which I once would have clung to or averted my eyes from. Finally, it seems, I don't require anything from him to complete me.

Maybe I feel this way because, on the afternoon of the day my son left, I read straight through the poems of my anthology for the first time and felt myself to be in a community of shared experience, in a conversation at last. Nothing to feel self-conscious or self-effacing about in this embrace of acceptance and understanding. Thank goodness, of course, for all I've learned from therapy, from Buddhist thought about non-clinging, from Alanon's prodding toward detachment, and from 70 years of living. Thank goodness, now, for the solace and comfort of these poems, these poet parents whose children have grown up.

I've gathered the poems in *Family Reunion* primarily from extensive reading in the published works of contemporary poets whom I knew had adult children and by soliciting poems from my own network of mature men and women poets. I selected these poems from three hundred or so candidates because I like each one very much and because they fit the scope of this anthology. I'm sorry there are only six poems by fathers. I wish I'd found more that were as good.

I am happy with the effect of these poems on each other as they cover much of the continuum of experiences and feelings we share as parents of grown children: The perils and joys of connection – so many visits and phone calls! Pain for terrible misfortune that has happened. Fear for what might happen. Acknowledgment of our own imperfections and helplessness. The rare achievement of non-attachment. The maturity of the parent, still sheltering, but with open arms, wiser now, finally "grown up." I am struck by the fact that these are all primarily love poems. There is little despair here. Always there is a healing, a holding together in the face of *life as it is*. In the mysterious way of all creation, these poems are comforting. They say what can't be said any other way.

Sondra Zeidenstein
Goshen, Connecticut
July 2000 – July 2001

Notes:

1. The PBS documentary, *First Person Plural*, can be viewed by going online to http://www.pbs.org/pov/filmarchive and locating it in the archives of the series called *Point of View*.

2. *Going on being* is the theme of a book of the same name by Mark Epstein, a psychotherapist who is also a Buddhist. The phrase has to do with living freshly in the present, not being emotionally stuck in the narrative of one's life.

3. I cannot locate the issue of *Ms.* in which this essay appeared but it can probably be located by going online to the archives of the magazine at http://www.msmagazine.com

4. The interview with Tema Nason, edited into narrative form, appears in *Full Moon*, a chapbook of her stories published by Chicory Blue Press in 1993 and, also, in *The Crimson Edge: Older Women Writing, Volume One* (Chicory Blue Press, 1996). *Full Moon* can be ordered by visiting the website http://www.chicorybluepress.com or from http://www.amazon.com

5. In *Sula* by Toni Morrison (Plume, 1982), pp.71-2.

6. In *Woman: An Intimate Geography* by Natalie Angier (Houghton Mifflin, 1999), p.319.

7. In *A General Theory of Love* by Lewis, Amini and Lannon (Vintage, 2001) p.95.

8. After creating and naming this anthology, I came across and enjoyed reading a non-fiction book, *Family Re-Union: Reconnecting Parents and Children in Adulthood*, by Robert Kuttner and Sharland Trotter (Simon & Shuster, 2002). It is a very informative and, at the same time, accessible and deeply humane book about the potentials of relationships between parents and grown children. It summarizes and integrates recent important psychological thought on this subject and includes a good bibliography.

Table of Contents

Family Reunion

Grace Paley

For My Daughter

I wanted to bring her a chalice
or maybe a cup of love
or cool water   I wanted to sit
beside her as she rested
after the long day   I wanted to adjure
commend   admonish   saying don't
do that   of course   wonderful   try
I wanted to help her grow old   I wanted
to say last words   the words famous
for final enlightenment   I wanted
to say them now   in case I am in
calm sleep when the last sleep strikes
or aged into disorder   I wanted to
bring her a cup of cool water

I wanted to explain   tiredness is
expected   it is even appropriate
at the end of the day

Elizabeth Claman

The Queens of Ice Cream

"What a mother you were!"
You shake your head, laughing.

I'm visiting for Christmas
and we're curled together on your grown-up bed,
two spoons and a quart of pistachio between us,
remembering the day,
almost twenty years before,
we drove 40 miles to the beach and back,

stopping at every ice cream store we saw,
eating almond fudge, tin roof, lime sherbet, rocky road,
sticky with it. Not able to get enough.
You, six, and me, just past my teens.

Sand in our hair, and sunburns.
Hot Santa Ana wind through the sun roof,
rock 'n' roll on the radio,
and both of us shouting and pointing.
"There's another," and "Another!"
        and "Another!"

Melissa Shook

The Real Story

"I could never have slept
with him," you say
from three thousand miles.
"I'm not
criticizing but you must
have hated
yourself
to do it."
How can I tell her
what her father once was,
gifted, elegant,
pale brown skin,
that occasional smile.
I walked past him
through swinging doors
carrying heavy trays.
Princess of faculty dining
I remembered
who took coffee
with milk
and who drank tea.
Prince of all the rest,
tables of students,
the waiters he commanded
with a nod,
he sat aloof but
in control.
You tell me, "He's bald
and old and ugly
of character.
He was gone
before he went."
I want to

persuade you he was once
so fascinating
I never imagined
he'd even
talk to me.

The Ways of Daughters

My daughters are getting on.
They're in over their hips,
over their stretch marks.
Their debts are rising
and their faces are serious.

There are no great barns
or riding horses.
Only one of them has a washing machine.
Their old cars break
and are never fixed.

So what is this substance
that floods over them,
into which they wade
as if going out
to meet the Phoenicians?

And they have no nets
for those shifty-looking sailors.
But when I look again,
my daughters are alone in their kitchens.
Each child sweats in its junior bed.

And my girls are painting their fingernails.
They're rubbing lotions
on their impatient hands. This year
they are staining their hands and feet with henna.
They lie in the sun with henna packs on their hair.

Insomnia

in a dark room the dial glows 4:44
three 4's with open arms
like the cactus *saguaro*
that grows in the southwest
and I'm happy
I'll be seeing my daughter tomorrow
two northerners
one from the east one from the west
in neutral territory
Arizona
        where the spiny
open-armed cactus dwells.
Saguaro. Joy. Reunion. Sleep

Family Reunion

The week in August you come home,
adult, professional, aloof,
we roast and carve the fatted calf
– in our case home-grown pig, the chine
garlicked and crisped, the applesauce
hand-pressed. Hand-pressed the greengage wine.

Nothing is cost-effective here.
The peas, the beets, the lettuces
hand sown, are raised to stand apart.
The electric fence ticks like the slow heart
of something we fed and bedded for a year,
then killed with kindness's one bullet
and paid Jake Mott to do the butchering.

In winter we lure the birds with suet,
thaw lungs and kidneys for the cat.
Darlings, it's all a circle from the ring
of wire that keeps the raccoons from the corn
to the gouged pine table that we lounge around
distressed before any of you was born.

Benign and dozy from our gluttonies,
the candles down to stubs, defenses down,
love leaking out unguarded the way
juice dribbles from the fence when grounded
by grass stalks or a forgotten hoe,
how eloquent, how beautiful you seem!

Wearing our gestures, how wise you grow,
ballooning to overfill our space,
the almost-parents of your parents now.
So briefly having you back to measure us
is harder than having let you go.

Betty Buchsbaum

Morning Visit

I lie down with my exhausted Susan
whose infant sleeps in the crib beside us.
All night she wailed, a broken siren.
I say yes, I'm tired too, so she won't be tempted
to talk, drink tea with me in the kitchen.
She fluffs my pillow, lies so near I breathe
on her closed eye-lids. Inhaling baby pee
and apricot oil, I drowse back to a morning
she visited her 94-year-old grandmother.
Finding her propped in bed, eating breakfast
from a tray, my daughter kicked off her shoes,
climbed in under the covers and shared
the toast and coffee. I see her snuggled
against a white eyelet nightgown, ruffled
at the neck and bulged by a colostomy bag.
She strokes her grandmother's thin white hair,
once a heavy, hip-length mane she was allowed
to braid, unbraid on summer visits.
Urine, powder, rubbing alcohol, overheated air –
the sweet-stale-sour odor of the old and newborn,
my daughter's arm trails across my thickening midriff.
Her fingers curl, long and graceful tendrils,
around my bony, liver-spotted hand.

Visiting My Formerly Runaway Daughter and Her Husband at the Orchard in Vermont

Let's drink to the hard-working people;
Let's drink to the salt of the earth.
                        – *The Rolling Stones*

I need to explain to myself, so I tell my friends
you've dropped out of the middle class after one
short generation – mine, which rose on the spines
of workingclass parents. Out of their neighborhoods,
their tax brackets, their broken English.

When I arrive up the dirt road, having stopped
for more detailed directions at the orchard
packing house, and having made nonetheless
one wrong turn, one stop at the wrong white
house, you are waiting. For me, and for
him, your husband two hours overdue, gone fishing.
Oh daughter of the strong arm and sunburned nose.
Oh child of my disorderly bosom.
I am glad to sit at your sticky table,
glad to drink the strong coffee you've brewed,
you remember my addiction.

We hear an engine panting uphill and then he
and his fishing mate, Larry from Florida,
reel into the kitchen, bravely displaying one
8-inch fish of unknown origin. Larry is happy,
and your man heavy-lidded – maybe there has been beer –
and when Larry smiles and speaks, his top teeth wag.
I can't understand more than one word in his ten
but his smile says fine, and I shake his hand
as calloused as my stone-carving, window-cleaning,
metal-lathing father's. Your Bobby gets Larry
to clean the fish, to show him how, and when

Carole Simmons Oles

the dirty job is done – we three have turned
squeamish from the lesson – Bobby wraps
the fish in the daily newspaper
and throws it into the freezer, where intaglio
stories of x's drunk-driving charge, y's
nine-pound boy, will solidify on its flank.

More coffee, Larry's departure, and a plan:
a tour of the orchard, the hidden sauna, the stream
then blueberry picking. But first
a snack of blueberries you two
have already gathered, set like sapphires
in vanilla yogurt unintentionally frozen. Delicious,
delicious, and you, child, by my side.

We stalk the rows of blueberry bushes, finding
what remains this late. The knock each globe
makes against cardboard reminds me of Sal's pail
in her story we read, heads touching over the page.
So many berries left, I am amazed
as we three spread out, calling to each other
from our separate camouflaging rows of green.
So many, and some so fat I can't believe
birds overlooked them, can't resist eating
them under the sun, under the pure blue of our reunion.
We combine our pickings – one luscious load –
and drive back to the bunkhouse.

The two Bartlett pears on your windowsill
lean onto each other's shoulders like lovers.
They are almost ready, one is blushing, the light
forms an aura around them. One stands straighter,
seems to hold the other up more, but may
need the other's leaning to have it seem so.

Carole Simmons Oles

With dinner at the Jade Wah, we cannot
drink water because the supply is ruined
by industry. We wonder about the ice
in our soft drinks. I tell you of dark figures
squatting in ditches along the road from the airport
into the city of Calcutta; of your father fainting
on the bathroom tiles…Your father –
we blink once and pass him.
Last time we ate here, two summers ago, you
were living in a shack with six other people
and came to dinner barefoot. The management never flinched.

We reject our fortunes, rush down the highway
to the cinema to see "Parenthood." You sit between us
holding hands with Bobby and me, as onscreen
families sandpaper each other. One daughter
wears your name, and elopes. Her parents are
divorced; the father, a dentist, loves his hand on the drill.
Neither of us is conned by the ending: a baby
for each happy pair. Retrograde, we agree.

Back in the bunkhouse, your boss and two other pickers
sit at the kitchen table and kibbitz.
Paul has just returned from 3 months on a fishing boat
off the Aleutians and Terri, who smiles like a horizon,
follows crops across the continent.
Your boss says I look like your older sister.
I squirm when he jokes about elopement, cigarette breaks.
Soon it's bedtime – early. Works starts in the coolest
morning hours. You've made me a place upstairs:
a mattress on a boxspring on the floor. Across the hall,
you and Bobby will watch from your bed
sunrise over Monadnock. From my corner I see the shapes
of apple trees beyond the glass, silvered. I sleep.

By 5:30 the pans are rattling. Bobby cooks
blueberry pancakes so full of berries they clump
in the pan. He complains. I enjoy them. Good, strong
coffee and if I didn't have to leave, I'd stay,
try to pick apples. I don't want this to end now,
as I hug my girl and her husband.
I don't want them all to pile into the free,
battered Ford Fiesta, to follow them down
the rutted hill, out to the stop sign
she drives toward too fast,
to the packing house where they turn left
to get their orders for the day,
where she waves her hand out the window, her hand
toward which I, continuing straight, wave mine.

Pittsburgh

And my beautiful daughter
had her liver cut open in Pittsburgh.
My god, my god! I rubbed
her back over the swollen and wounded
essentiality, I massaged
her legs, and we talked of death.
At the luckiest patients with liver cancer have
a 20% chance. We might have talked
of my death, not long to come. But no,
the falling into death of a beautiful
young woman is so much more important.
A wonderful hospital. If I must die
away from my cat Smudge and my Vermont Castings stove
let it be at Allegheny General.
I read to her, a novella by Allan Gurganus,
a Russian serious flimsiness by Voinovich,
and we talked. We laughed. We actually
laughed. I bought her a lipstick
which she wore though she disliked the color.
Helicopters took off and landed on the hospital pad,
bringing hearts and kidneys and maybe livers
from other places to be transplanted
into people in the shining household of technology
by shining technologists, wise and kindly.
The chances are so slight. Oh, my daughter,
my love for you has burgeoned –
an excess of singularity ever increasing –
you are my soul – for forty years. You
still beautiful and young. In my hotel
I could not sleep. In my woods, on my
little farm, in the blizzard on the mountain,
I could not sleep either, but scribbled
fast verses, very fast and
wet with my heartsblood and brainjuice

Hayden Carruth

all my life, as now
in Pittsburgh. I don't know which of
us will live the longer, it's all a flick
of the wrist of the god mankind invented
and then had to deinvent, such a failure, like all
our failures, and the worst and best
is sentimentality after all. Let us go out together.
Here in brutal Pittsburgh. Let us
be together in the same room,
the old poet and the young painter,
holding hands, a calm touch, a whisper,
as the thumping helicopters go out and come in,
we in the crisis of forever inadequately medicated
pain, in the love of daughter and father.

14

Television War

for David

Thirty-eight hours in
and we change the channel
to game shows or soaps, anything
to divert our attention.
Those first horrifying hours –
CNN reporting bombs over Baghdad,
no-one could lift their eyes from the screen,

all of us sick in the stomach –
Arabs falling to their prayer mats,
the air humming above Baghdad.
A bomb spirals a white hiss upward,
streets blacken with blood and debris.
This is television war, unreal as a video game,
every kid watching holding a joystick.

In this house we hug the TV,
unable to breathe or turn away,
blessed if we are asleep in our chairs
while our son's ship slips into the Gulf,
the screen blue and flickering.

The Moment

While my tires were being rotated I waited inside a dim garage
three steps from the light of day. Across the street a cement house
    baked
in full sun. Its white roof wavered in the heat. Behind it another roof.
And then the steeple of a sad church with red glass windows.
Not a bird, nor a cloud was in sight. But a man on a silver bike passed.
And a black couple, backs to me, pushed a stroller across four lanes
    of traffic.
They waved to a man sitting in shadow beside the cement house.

All that, I wrote in a letter to my boy – a slice of home. I wished
to send more, reassurance that things are as he left them.
It isn't true. The man I saw in shadow has deserted
his post, leaving his chair tipped against the house, striding away
on ground that has never known landmines.

Last week I sent a package with books and CDs but no strawberry cake.
Today while my tires were rotated I watched the red hand sweep
the moment when somewhere in Bosnia a Guardsman from South
    Carolina

my only son, turned twenty-one.

Victoria Wyttenberg

The Joyce Hotel

Night thickens around drab buildings
as I walk to the desk and pay the 1st night
for my son, and a key fine from last time.
Three people at most could fit into this space,
and the night clerk, a man with gray hair to his collar
and a soft felt hat. Rates posted by the desk,
by the day or week, front door open 24 hours,
security camera. One visitor allowed in the room
at a time, charge for overnight. No pets.

No drugs. Clean linen for a price.
Five years ago Michael died here,
a bottle still in his hand.
My son meets me, hunkered down
in his black coat and we walk three blocks
where I buy him soup. He eats every bite
and all the bread. He is a long way from curls
and the crib, from the boy in blue shorts
opening his hand to feed the giraffe.

Everything behind a loss,
not much ahead he can see that seems worth
this enormous effort, everything he owns
in one duffle bag.
This hotel keeps beds for those who dream
of better times, beds stained and cold,
beds of disordered and sleepless nights,
beds for those who lie curled in their own misfortune,
those who reach out and find nothing
but stale air, beds for those with hearts worn down.

Victoria Wyttenberg

Where is God in this picture? In the wool
of my son's coat? In small lights of the city?
In the potatoes and onions in the soup?
And what of the man sleeping on the steps
next door? How do we ever know
what helps and what brings us to our knees?

Men stand in groups along the street and one man
walks alone. If anyone notices they must think
us an odd pair, a short 60 year old woman, a young man,
tall and thin, shadows under eyes.
No moon tonight with its old scarred face.

Winter Heart

Across our northern land, chickadees,
worn out from tireless labor,
fall asleep with their hats on.

Crows roost in groups of two or more.
Predators to young robins and songbirds,
crows are prey to Great Horned Owls,
who eat only the brains.

. . .

The wind blows cold enough to crack,
and a December moon holds the new moon
in her arms, as I once cradled my grown
son, Michael. Abhorring our wasteful

culture, he now lives his private vow
of poverty, raids dumpsters for his daily
greens, knows who discards what and when.

It's harder in winter, he says, *since fresh
things freeze so fast.* Last summer, behind
the café where he worked, we loaded my car

with tables and blankets, left behind
by fleeing drug dealers, then drove
to Cedar Lake, where he carried our cache

to the homeless camp hidden in the woods.
They'd lost the bridge they slept under
when police drilled holes so rainwater

Jill Breckenridge

dripped through. *Shelters aren't safe,*
he said, *especially for teenage kids.*

Today Michael carries, from our house,
black candlesticks, made in Kenya, to light
his table, a block from a crack house.

He has also taken the remains of our
holiday almonds, which he'll divide
and gift-wrap for homeless kids, sleeping
in their own shelters he helped provide.

. . .

Thousands of Alaskan moose, driven
by winter's tyranny, migrate to lower
land, where, in search of food, over

a hundred have been hit by trains,
and so many killed by cars,
officials have stopped counting.

. . .

On Christmas evening, we bring sugar cookies
to our daughter, who nurses her December baby.
We watched the baby's entrance into this world,
head, as it crowned, soft as a water balloon,

then a baby girl popped out, part fish,
part bird, but fully human, formed, then painted
for her entry with her mother's blood.

. . .

It all depends on what the heart is able
to encompass beyond its own singular beat.

In the cold December air, hearts of sleeping
chickadees beat over 500 times a minute,

twice that when they're awake. They survive
the fiercest winter, live only a year.

    . . .

In New York city, on Christmas morning,
our son, Mark, volunteers at the AIDS ward
for prisoners and the homeless. One prisoner

confides he can't celebrate Christmas.
He doesn't understand why he, of all people,
got AIDS, or why he ended up in jail.

He doesn't deserve to die; he didn't rob
that store. *I'm innocent,* he repeats.

    . . .

Though the radio predicts a storm,
at this moment, we can easily count
every star within our range of vision.

Soon it will snow again, softening
the harsh winter landscape. Some trucks
will plow, others will salt against ice.

That night, on roads clear for our safe
passage, moose will come forth slowly,

like prehistoric dreams from deep
in the soul of the forest. While we
sleep, they will kneel to the salt.

Elizabeth Shelley

Son Suspended

roof high, knocks
down decking,
hangs from clouds
by a hammer claw.
I turn on music,
to wall out his din
of sound and no sound:
steady slam of mallet,
crack and clap of falling
wood, syncopation of long
silences. I strain to keep
fluid in the movement
of my day, to flow
past pinnings of maternal fear:
a son's fall from roofline
to concrete, tree limb to garden,
cradle to rug.

Alice Ryerson Hayes

Imagining Water

My daughter lives among the dry
gray green chamiso bushes
on the banks of a river of sand.
Every day she walks up it
towards mountains, and every day
she walks back down to her children
waiting on the banks of the dry arroyo.

I tell my friend and she says:
What about flash floods?
So I begin imagining water rushing,
flinging stones, throwing my daughter
over its torrential shoulders
while her children cry on the banks.

I telephone my daughter in New Mexico
to warn her before it's too late.
She laughs, the way people in deserts
laugh at the idea of water. "And anyway"
she says, "my arroyo doesn't run
in a canyon. I'd just step out of the way."

Visual Ritual

Black winter nights
the heat rises
and the old windows rattle,
when I get into bed
under the stars
of my doubled quilts,
close my eyes and envision
the wealth of your hair, your
sweeping smile, the delicate inset
of your bones, hands, as ever,
in pockets, sweet
eyes, nose and mouth
your father passed down,

and I lift up my palms
and pull through my mind
the far spheres
that service this world,
pull a funnel of splendor,
spark and scintilla, flicker
and blaze, pull it down
in a vertical white figure eight,
pour it over your head,

then I orbit the circuits,
all boundaries subsumed
in one shielded zone.
Crown, neck and shoulders,
chest, belly, buttocks,
thighs, knees and shins.
And ankles, and heels
in one spiral coil
lazered to dazzle –

the love of a mother
who from this distance
with *this* keeps you safe,
as she must
let you go.

Pearl Garrett Crayton

Laughter from the Sky

I heard laughter falling from the sky,
tumbling down on my bare head,
much too close for me to imagine
that it came from angels frolicking among the clouds,
laughter tumbling down to hurt me.
I looked up and my heart stopped.
There on the ridge of our house
I saw my only sons walking,
laughing, frolicking with Death.

Frozen with fear, I watched,
knowing that if I called out
for them to come down,
this might frighten them.
They would lose their balance,
and Lord only knows what then.
So I stood there, hoping that they would see me.
Soon they did, and they came down.
The oldest one told me, "See, Mommee.
We can climb Daddee's ladder
and walk on houses, too. We're big boys now."

I heard laughter falling down from the sky.
I looked up and saw my only sons
trying to walk on the ridge of our world
while invectives from racists rang out,
deriding them for trying to climb higher
than the world allowed their kind.
Standing on solid ground, I wait,
hoping that they will not get frightened by the din,
hoping that they will see me standing there
to catch them if they fall, and if not,
to gather up their broken bodies
and carry them safely home.

Marie Ponsot

"Love is not Love"

*For Elena Cornaro, first woman Ph.D., born
in Padua, 1647; and for those whose children
are in pain here and now*

It is cold. I am
drawing my life around me to get warm.
Holes in the blanket can't be re-woven.
Some thorns caught in it still scratch. Some tear.

I reach for comfort
to the left-out lives of women here and gone.
They lend them willingly. They know my need.
They do not hate me for crying. It beats despair.

Elena Cornaro
hands me her cinderella cap & gown.
I put them on. Stiff fur. But intact: she
(when eleven! just in time) saw

in a flash the mortal needles
their rain of cupidity
aimed at eyes across the looking air,

laughed and in singleness averted them
shielded by choice against the dark & steel.
She stopped herself in herself, refined
her will, and brought her mind virgin to bear

stretched across nine languages – nine sun-
keepers, their word-clusters grapes
of intellect, for wine
she pours me now.

Marie Ponsot

It stings like speed:
Ph.D., TB, breath on fire, young,
she sported her doctoral vair
in vain. She too died of blood.
Yet the mind she trained
had warmed her in the storm
(all storms one storm) where
she'd left no hostage howling to be freed,
no captive mouths to feed;
in her sight, no punctual winter swarm
of guilt – pale bees whose attack breeds
paralysis, and dread of snow
that masks the snare.
I am stuck in cold. It is deaf. It is eiron.

What has happened to my child
is worse than I can tell you
and I'm ashamed to say
is more than I can bear.

Elena, listen.
My body speaks nine languages but the greed
of me is stuck, my exposed eyes prickle,
I think blank, he's lost out there, I'm scared.

What I have borne, I bear.

Oh I praise your continence, kind life, pure form.
Your way's one way, not mine; you're summer-stopped;
my meadow's mud, turned stone in this icy air.

Whose fault is it? It's at the root my fault.
But in your cape, I come to?
And I'm in your care?
As he is mine, so I am yours to bear
alive. He is still alive. He has not died of it.
Wronged. Wrong.

Regardless love is hard to bear.
It has no hospital.
It is its own fireplace.
All it takes is care.

Well, when you grew intimate with pain,
what did you do. How did you do it. Where.
That, this? Thanks. Suppose I'm not in time.
Is it worth a try. I'll try,

try to conceive of room to spare,
a surround of walls steady and steadying
an uncracked ceiling & a quiet floor,
a morning room, a still room
where we'd bring mind to bear upon
our consequences – we who make
no difference, who ignoring
absence of response have chosen
ways to love we can't go back on
and we won't,

regardless:
like your holy aura, Elena,
like your singleness, my fertility,
your tiny eminence, your early death;

like our Vassar Miller, her persistent listening;
like our Tillie Olsen, her persistent flowering;
like our Djuna and our Emily
their insolent beauty visored,
disguised as hermit crabs;
like our Sarah Jewett's faithful gaze –
cast down –
like my long-drawn-out mistakes.

Elena maybe we
remember each other as room
for when to cry, what to cry for,
cry to whom.

Clean Plate

That flowery winter in California
when I spent the better part of an afternoon
clipping, raking, piling debris in your yard
you could barely thank me (as if I needed thanks) (I
need thanks) it was hard
to hear you explain that everything I do is a way of
saying you'd failed. Even mopping the kitchen floor or
how I kept on sweeping the dining room was abuse.
What to do? Leave? No. I said I didn't mean what you
took me to mean. You said "Listen.
You don't listen." I shut up. You looked
furious, then sad. And we both cried. That night
I cooked chicken paprika and although dinner was
too late and Elijah fussed, we sat down together
quietly. You served the wine.
                    I was glad you ate
with gusto, even (as we used to say
when you were 5) "cleaned your plate."

Pat Schneider

Don't Look at the Moon

You talk to your daughter
about her divorce. She says
I have to leave this place;
there are memories everywhere.

You listen.
You can hear the green plant growing
in the sunlight in her window.
At night she tells you
don't look at the moon.
It's too beautiful, riding
the black oak branches.

She is packing her bags to go.
All that you know is not enough.

Marilyn Hacker

Grief

for Iva

I
You turned twenty and your best friend died
a week after your birthday, in a car
on a bright icy morning. Now you are
flying home. I called, you called back. You howled; you cried
like the child you probably ceased to be
the moment that I told you she was dead –
your anchor, homegirl, unsolicited
sister.
       Now you are standing in front of me,
tall and in tears and I have nothing to say.
You're too big for me to hold in my skinny arms,
but I do, windbreaker, backpack and all,
stroke snow-splotched wet hair you probably chewed in a storm
of tears in the cab. Your garment bag leans on the wall,
a black dress in it.
              Now I am watching you growing away
from me, toward hours in a car you and two friends drive
through the same treacherous snow, to empty her dorm
room, to sit with the injured boy, wired and re-formed
in plaster, weeping because he was still alive;
toward where you never would have expected to come
to see your friend, or what briefly remained of your friend
thin and naked under a sheet, the wound
at her temple inconsequential-looking (a slight
line of dried blood from her ear) stopped still on a white
marble slab in a crematorium.

II
Your great-aunts, centenarian-and-some,
write their memoirs. Stroke-silenced, your grandmother
turned eighty in a Brooklyn nursing home,
looking as if she might stand up, recover
her thoughts, her coat, and walk off toward the L

34

train – though she won't. Chemo has let me live
so far. Some fluke, prudence or miracle
has kept your father seronegative.
The January day they called you out
of computer lab so you could phone
home, I'm sure you ran your cursor down
a list of possible mortalities,
guessing it was death you were called about,
assuming that it would be one of these.

III
Your "black dress" was the velvet skirt you wear
for choir recitals. K. J., who stood behind
you at the door, her coat still on, her hands
empty and open, met you at the air-
port, since I was sick. Your grief came in
to us like another illness, one which we
could hardly palliate with soup and tea,
which didn't stop me from making tea again
when I could let you go.
                        But you had gone
farther away, to where she was a light
receding as you watched, to where she was
teasing you on the train to Argelès,
to where she left you at the bus stop ten
days ago, to where she glaringly was not.

IV
I booked you three at the Hôtel Malher:
sixth floor, no bath, a hundred-fifty francs.
You crowded on my couch, made phone calls, drank
tea, took turns showering and washing hair.
You'd had breakfast. You'd gone to the bank.
You were all seventeen. A girl in Tours,

her pen pal, had invited you to come
down for the weekend. You would take the train.
And then you'd take the train to Perpignan.
Was there a train from Tours to Perpignan?
Her mother's (gay) friend had a summer home
in Argelès, had offered the spare room.
(I think I had to route you through Bordeaux.)
You knew your way, some, from years I'd ferried you
over, "Unaccompanied," to France.
She'd spent six exchange months in Budapest,
could be acute about the difference,
but mostly loved the light, the river, under
the influence...The boy seemed youngest,
and anything *she* liked, except museums,
he was willing to attest was wonder-
ful too. Like colts, like April trees, your threesome
bristled with innocence and confidence.
A sprained ankle, lost camera, missed train
were the mishaps that you thought to fear.
I sent you out into the summer rain
between your junior and your senior year.

V

A crowd, standing room only, turned out for
her funeral. Masses of wasted flowers
embraced a photo album you'd spent hours
assembling, through the night and dawn, with her
shell-shocked kid sister. Then you'd gone together
to face your first cadaver, and belief
in the obscenity that caused your grief.
The obsequies of a dead senator
might not have brought out such a throng, I said,
standing in line, waiting my turn to view
family snapshots: mother and infant, two-

year-old walking, standing on her head
at eight: domestic Sunday afternoon
pastime turned into mourning. She herself
was now a box of ashes on a shelf
whose sixteen-year-old shadow mugged at you
next to a Beatles poster in your blue
disheveled bedroom as you took that one.

Cortney Davis

How I Imagine It

Ahead of me on the road, my daughter
and her husband in their old Subaru.
He's driving and I'm following them to the Danbury garage
to fix the ping that's been there for weeks
when suddenly their car careens, crashes into a tree
and bursts into flames. I park my car, just stop it, and run,
run to the door bashed off its frame.
My hands reach in, carefully,
across her silky printed dress, the white-collared one
she likes so much. She is thin
and graceful, I unhook her seatbelt,
the silver metal clasp snaps open and the webbing falls away,
her head tilted as if she's sleeping,
but I smell gas, the stink of burning tires.
People cry out, shouting to me *Get away!* I lean in,
incredibly strong, and lift her up and out, she is all air,
long arms, hands with my knucklebones.
I hold her, wrap her dress around her knees,
her husband lies over the steering wheel, the horn blasting,
like in the movies, and I run, holding her in my arms.
I kneel by the roadside, let her body unfold
in a tree's green shadow, into long stems that smell like cut grass
the summers my father pushed the handmower and mother
made lemonade, squeezing the lemons in her hands, picking
each seed out. I bend,
knowing if I can save her, I can save myself, if I save her
she will forgive me for everything I have done,
for everything I have allowed to be done. I bend,
place my mouth over hers, take in one big breath, breathe it
into her mouth, into lungs that catch, grab it,
hurl it through to her heart, her heart
holds and contracts, once, again, again and she gasps for air.

I feel her warm, every cell ignites and glows, she is
alive....The light
turns yellow, turns red. Their car slows ahead of me, stops.
The stoplight swings in the wind. It's almost Autumn.

Raymond Carver

To My Daughter

Everything I see will outlive me. – Anna Akhmatova

It's too late now to put a curse on you – wish you
plain, say, as Yeats did his daughter. And when
we met her in Sligo, selling her paintings, it'd worked –
she *was* the plainest, oldest woman in Ireland.
But she was safe.
For the longest time, his reasoning
escaped me. Anyway, it's too late for you,
as I said. You're grownup now, and lovely.
You're a beautiful drunk, daughter.
But you're a drunk. I can't say you're breaking
my heart. I don't have a heart when it comes
to this booze thing. Sad, yes, Christ alone knows.
Your old man, the one they call Shiloh, is back
in town, and the drink has started to flow again.
You've been drunk for three days, you tell me,
when you know goddamn well drinking is like poison
to our family. Didn't your mother and I set you
example enough? Two people
who loved each other knocking each other around,
knocking back the love we felt, glass by empty glass,
curses and blows and betrayals?
You must be crazy!
Wasn't all that enough for you?
You want to die? Maybe that's it. Maybe
I think I know you, and I don't.
I'm not kidding, kiddo. Who are you kidding?
Daughter, you can't drink.
The last few times I saw you, you were out of it.
A cast on your collarbone, or else
a splint on your finger, dark glasses to hide
your beautiful bruised eyes. A lip
that a man should kiss instead of split.
Oh, Jesus, Jesus, Jesus Christ!
You've got to take hold now.

40

Raymond Carver

Do you hear me? Wake up! You've got to knock it off
and get straight. Clean up your act. I'm asking you.
Okay, telling you. Sure, our family was made
to squander, not collect. But turn this around now.
You simply must – that's all!
Daughter, you can't drink.
It will kill you. Like it did your mother, and me.
Like it did.

Rise and Shine

What you miss most, you say, is how each morning he'd say
rise and shine, and now it's over.

I remain silent. Your mother, I'm glad to hear this man is gone,
yet I want another to love you,

to cherish you in so ordinary a way that what you miss are first words
singing your eyes open.

At thirty you've had almost no men in your life. I never taught you
to flirt, you say.

Of course not! I wanted you to have more than marriage, be more than
a baby having a baby. Your glow

in this new time would take you wherever you wanted to go. The world
had come round: Rise and shine

a woman could. You were born to it, the door *past* the kitchen. Endowed,
your giggle, your wit, your dance

insured your miraculous heart's survival, I thought, until you confided
a repetitive dream: your flame

so small in a canvas of tar. Art talk I once would have relished. Now I
can't believe I pray someone else will come

Myra Shapiro

to love you. I'm frightened by your dullness; I'm frightened by
your sleep. I can't believe we're stuck

in an old story. Must a prince appear? Must I die first? I want my life.
    Please
rise and shine.

Letter: Thursday, 16 September

Today is the day I took the father of my grandboy & girl into the clinic for the doctor to look at his wounded foot. He had put a nail All The Way Through It. What kind of man does that? A man whose mind is elsewhere. Maybe a man who is worried. Or scared. I don't know. After, coming back to their house, I held the baby for a long time. Ariana. She is two months old tomorrow. I never told you about her birth. A home birth. Two midwives & me & the other grandma. I never told you how she was born a dusky stone blue, a small sculpture perfectly composed, hands folded over her chest like the old pictures of saints. She was born just after we heard the church bells ring noon. Her mother, my Heidi, was strong and able. But toward the end her eyes, my Heidi's eyes, were the eyes of an animal. Pure pain. I held her gaze. We did that. We did not flinch. I've not turned to look at this again until this moment. I didn't expect to do it now. Here. On this Thursday. On this page.

What I Need To Tell You

At 45, you find yourself in this marriage –
his temper, his volatility, his addiction.
The children don't understand and you can't explain,
because neither do you. How did you get here?
Why do you stay? This much you know:
a home shouldn't be a minefield.

Look at where you came from. Your parents wedded
to a delusion: we were a perfect family. Your father
orphan, playmeister, trying to figure out how to be.
I, being who I was as a child, a responsible adult.
You, blond braided, curled up in the blue wing chair
reading, learned very young that what didn't fit
the myth wasn't true.

It never occurred to me that a mother has to teach
her child to name her feelings. I was teaching you
not to. Dissonances dissolve by magic
through endurance.
"You are my best supporter," you tell me.
But who, what, how does love support, endure?

Greta Phinney

The Wedding Dress

What you chose
was so simple
and lovely
and elegant.
No false pearls
or imported lace,
no veil to conceal
or distract
from your face.

A simple statement
about the person
who will wear it
on her wedding day.

Beauty is not in a dress.

And I,
your mother,
sit in awe
that you could grow
up out of the imperfect
love I offered
to be so sure
that you are enough.
That love is enough,
that life is not a dress,
nor joy to be found
in such foolishness
as a price tag.

Greta Phinney

Nevertheless,
I would have bought
whatever dress
caught your eye,
without protest.

Diane Gregory

Not Putting Her Sick Dog to Sleep

How am I to hold you
over crackling miles
of telephone line.
Your message – a blur
of sobs and fractured words –
seems to be anguish
over a decision you've made –
a vote to delay loss.
What am I to do
my only beloved daughter
when your heartbreak
I cannot touch.
My arms are not long
enough to reach you
over a continent.
I cannot rock you
into a coping place.
There are no words – there never were –
to soothe your grieving –
Does this I worry
reverberate in your bones.
Your twice disturbed gestation
a mystery
until your too early birth
revealed
how the cord uniting us
was insecurely held.
You came home sickly.
I rocked and fed you
my breasts dripping milk.
You cried and cried
as if your life
depended on your wail.
And I felt fearful

Diane Gregory

for your life
as I do now
and helpless too –
your far away voice echoes
my anguish.
I have no words
to fulfill
your longing
for a mother
to make it all well
especially not this mother
myself so frail.

Long Distance Call from the Alone & Lonely

(for E)

Two thirty a.m. and I stumble through small dark rooms
toward the rasp of phone. Somewhere a dog's bark
sounds like it comes from deep inside a jar.

Her wailing probe, from years of paralysis, skewers me
each time. "What can I do with the rest of my life?"
Can she hear the dissolving of my heart? She hears
my silence.

"Are you there?" "Are you there?"

Finally I tell her the physical therapist should show her
how to transfer from bed to chair. He should show her,
free her.

"Should! Should! Should!" she throws back. "Oh, my God,
should!" Don't I understand? The government pays him nine
dollars an hour. She gets one hour. Don't I understand?

"It's not worth his while!" Then reality, my further disintegration:
There's no therapist, never was one.

It's always like this. We grapple with the unnamed until we
each hang up. Usually she calls back, apologizes, and then

gratefully our mouths will make cautious niceties, finally
declarations of love.

Usually she calls back. But this time while I wait in the dark
I know for a certainty I've understood nothing.
I've understood nothing for a very long time…

Hours after Her Phone Call

A freight train in the next county.
Three a.m. Even our screech owl asleep.
My husband breathes slow on the next pillow,
likewise the dog on her wicker couch.
The icebox trots overtime, shuts off.
Too soon in the year for crickets.
Only the appalling roar of moonlight
through white organdy, drip of a toilet
at the back of the house, too far to hear,
the spooked nickering of my grown daughter
across three thousand miles of dark,
that iron shoe in my heart.

Ferryboat

On the crowded ferryboat from Tortola to St. Thomas I sit behind
    my son
and when I'm not looking out at scrub forests on small mountains
or rows of timeshare condominiums set high over the water,
I study the back of his head with a claim not appropriate
when we are face to face and our eyes hold each other
no more than 2 or 3 seconds before they widen and turn away.
Does he feel his mother's eyes in his hair, buzzed up the neck like a
    wingtip collar,
on his neck burnt by the tropics, orderly pores, skin taut
except when he turns his head to watch the approach
to St. John's where he'll get off?
All that's left to see from the back are his ears, reddish and prominent,
the stiff way they stick out, perfectly aligned.
It's a wonder they didn't get clipped coming out of me.
I was screeching and swearing when this dark head crowned.
I bawled *fuck* and heard the nurses get very quiet.
Maybe I said, *fuck God.*
His head was a little bit squashed, pliable bone dented by forceps.
He hadn't much chin.
I gave up my separateness to protect him, we were one.
And now in the blue green water between sleeping volcanoes,
I can't see his future.
"Thank you for the good meals," he says on the dock.
"We'll be in touch," I say, imagining my palm on his breastbone.
He walks away.
Back on the boat, I take a seat in front, facing the stolid bulkhead,
stare at its signs about how many life preservers there are,
what sizes, where they are stored.

Ties

She wants to hang herself from the rafters, she says
to me at the top of the stairs, her arms billowing laundry's
just-from-the-dryer's cloud of heat. We make a frieze,

I'm so startled: blue jeans straggling down our only chute –
the steps – her hair hanging around her face like tangled wheat,
my breasts pushed against the banister. I'm thinking, What?

This was my glad girl. "You mean collar ties?", each visible 2 by 6
that keep the rafters from collapsing like piles of toothpicks
when snow thickens on shakes. She hasn't thought of the pitch

of the roof yet, its possibilities, although I see her struggling there,
her ankle shattered and white still falling, this daughter
who longed for wings climbing beyond the architecture

up past the icy line of the ridge where the stars fly: like those
that swayed from the mobile over her crib, like glittering ties
to the world above the world where whole countries

vanished beneath the jet she flew. Descended into her own
sorrow, she doesn't even fling the blue sheets down
to let me hold her close, desolate now and both of us alone.

Cortney Davis

The Ruined Boy

Already it has been slapped out of him –
all he has left is his long eyelashes.
Doesn't anyone else in the airport notice?
He glances down at his sneakers
and genuflects when his mama pokes him.
On the tarmac, men with shaved heads
zoom about with our luggage. Their boots
are thick-soled; do they love their mothers?
How about my son?
He doesn't wear glasses, like this boy,
and he's blonder than anyone waiting here.
When I'm home, we'll have dinner.
The kid with spectacles, I think,
will grow up to study finance in Cleveland.
How's work? I'll ask my son, trying to catch up.
He'll concentrate on his plate. I'll pick up the bill.

New Religion

Whom I have lost
somewhere in Canada
isn't my son
can't be, refuses to be
is a spirit man
instead
and tall
as before
reaching
not for love
but to fit
his spirit
with The Spirit
an idea seeming safe
or safer

so my not knowing
where he is
or how he is
is not deliberate cruelty
simply
his fear being
larger
than any way he has
of
knowing
my fear

Anorexia

Still, I'm the only one who might tell her.
Look at your thighs! Skinny as toothpicks!
She laughs me off, her thick-soled combat boots too big for her legs.
The whole of her maybe, *what, a size two?*
And the hair, long ringlets she dyed the color of eggplant.
Hungry? I ask, clattering dinner dishes, fanning the smells her way.
I'm offering dark bean soup, nachos with yellow cheese melting over
    the plate.
She stands like a sliver festering in an open wound.
When she turns to lift the kettle, to pour tea, add Nutrasweet, she
    almost disappears.
Where did you go, I shout.
The hot liquid gives her cramps.
She runs to the bathroom, comes back chewing Tums, Maalox,
    complaining.
It's hunger, I tell her, *not disease,* but she knows as well as I do.
I sit down, mouth watering, take large spoonfuls of soup, dip my
    bread.
She reads a magazine: the mannequins are thin as endive, their skin
    the color of cream.
When she turns to look at me again, I see a death mask.
Scooped out gourds where her eyes should be.
A smooth, domed bone of skull like the fragile skin of an egg.
She yawns, and I invent exotic desserts hidden inside her mouth.
One has thin pastry in layers, honey flowing from it.
The other is aflame – vanilla ice cream, cherries, chocolate sauces, a
    rich biscotti.
When she swallows, she makes glugging noises in her throat.
Dinner's almost over.
She goes to the refrigerator, opens the door.
Just looking?

She decides to brew more tea, turns the burner up until the kettle
    screams.
Frugal, she takes the used tea bag, dips it over and over into the new,
    boiling water.

New Mother

1

He has found a new mother
and I cannot hate him
when her name is Friend.
He has chosen carefully and well.
She listens and says Yes.

The joint she passes is fragrant and fat
an enticement to revelation
thin bridge to a tree-lined roadside
leaves hiding the sun
rocks set apart for a clear way.

He is moving to her land
and I cannot hate him
when its name is Fresh Start.
He has chosen or the land chose him.
The Smokers' Ball was *rad*
banners of cannabis floating
in the low winds off the canal.
The city will listen and say Yes.

The joint works faster than light.
This is great, he says, letting
his vampires float into ether
cops, neighbors, clients bugging him
don't forget the family
and death never coming to set
for a slow cigarette
on the next bench over.

Michele Cooper

2
The knife cuts just to the blood stripe
Candy sleeping in the bedroom
gin almost gone, boulders lifted.

But he is not going the distance
and I cannot hate him
when Death seems Friend.
It listens, hears,
beckons him to a fresh beginning
and rest.

The local grass isn't working
anyway, he's noticed,
and doesn't it rot when friends sour
off the vivid blues and greens?

3
My anguish hangs in the wind
and I cannot hate him
telling his stories in a new land
trials, nets, right, wrongs, and wringers.

The silver bird sweeps across the sea,
all baggage safely in the hold.

Raymond Carver

On an Old Photograph of My Son

It's 1974 again, and he's back once more. Smirking,
a pair of coveralls over a white tee-shirt,
no shoes. His hair, long and blond, falls
to his shoulders like his mother's did
back then, and like one of those young Greek
heroes I was just reading about. But
there the resemblance ends. On his face
the contemptuous expression of the wise guy,
the petty tyrant. I'd know that look anywhere.
It burns in my memory like acid. It's
the look I never hoped I'd live to see
again. I want to forget that boy
in the picture – that jerk, that bully!

What's for supper, mother dear? Snap to!
Hey old lady, jump, why don't you? Speak
when spoken to. I think I'll put you in
a headlock to see how you like it. I like
it. I want to keep you on
your toes. Dance for me now. Go ahead,
bag, dance. I'll show you a step or two.
Let me twist your arm. Beg me to stop, beg me
to be nice. Want a black eye? You got it!

Oh, son, in those days I wanted you dead
a hundred – no, a thousand – different times.
I thought all that was behind us. Who in hell
took this picture, and
why'd it turn up now,
just as I was beginning to forget?
I look at your picture and my stomach cramps.
I find myself clamping my jaws, teeth on edge, and
once more I'm filled with despair and anger.
Honestly, I feel like reaching for a drink.

Raymond Carver

That's a measure of your strength and power, the fear
and confusion you still inspire. That's
how mighty you once were. Hey, I hate this
photograph. I hate what became of us all.
I don't want this artifact in my house another hour!
Maybe I'll send it to your mother, assuming
she's still alive somewhere and the post can reach
her this side of the grave. If so, she'll have
a different reaction to it, I know. Your youth and
beauty, that's all she'll see and exclaim over.
My handsome son, she'll say. My boy wonder.
She'll study the picture, searching for her likeness
in the features, and mine. (She'll find them, too.)
Maybe she'll weep, if there are any tears left.
Maybe – who knows? – she'll even wish for those days
back again! Who knows anything anymore?

But wishes don't come true, and it's a good thing.
Still, she's bound to keep your picture out
on the table for a while and make over you
for a time. Then, soon, you'll go
into the big family album along with the other crazies –
herself, her daughter and me, her former husband. You'll be
safe in there, cheek to jowl with all your victims. But don't
worry, my boy – the pages turn, my son. We all
do better in the future.

Carrie Allen McCray

Letter to a Son I Once Knew

(postmarked May 1974)

Child of the mind
altering sixties,
where have you gone?
you used to walk
wet-faced into
the wind,
your little black
dog beside you
both sloshing into
the house
leaving mud-marks
on a freshly
scrubbed floor
Home from college
we sat together
sharing the philosophies
of Dubois, King, Fanon
Thoreau and Malcolm;
you, sifting out
the words
that shaped your own
I see you now
Tall, handsome in
your airforce uniform,
a sensitive young man
looking out the
kitchen window
asking of war
Is this the answer –
then you went away
I searched for you
in many light and
lovely places
where still rings

Carrie Allen McCray

the sound of your
laughter
but did not find
you there,
changing course,
I walked the
lonely paths of
war torn, drug
shattered youth
saw huddled in a
deep, dark corner
a stranger, his
eyes closed, his
head down on his
knees
Who was that?
slowly your lifted
eyes told me
For one fleeting
moment you returned
the flicker of your
old smile,
small light in an
otherwise abyss
But I'll keep searching,
my child of the sixties,
Knowing that there
in the eye of the
hurricane, deep
in the center
of you, is the
son I once knew.

Balm
(1/20/02)

> *There is a balm in Gilead*
> *That makes the wounded whole...* *

Apprehension, a heavy cloak,
I travel the distance to see you,
    car to bus,
      bus to subway,
        subway to Long Island,
          cab to Sunrise Manor.
Unseasonably warm, this day is beautiful,
  yet what will it be like?
Mercurial, your troubled mind.

Relieved, I find a calmness in you.
  You do not turn me away
as you have done so many times
  when in your "other world."

We sit together now in the garden
  and talk of many things,
hard to believe you're almost sixty.
  The sun shines silver
on your graying hair.

Your deep voice and laughter
  reminiscent of earlier times,
times when you were vibrant,
  loved life, dabbled in art, wrote poetry,
times when we enjoyed talking about
  family, philosophy and politics,
times when we solved the problems
  of the world.

Carrie Allen McCray

You speak now of your roommate
   "He's old and sickly," you say,
"so I try to help him all I can,"
   your sensitive side resurfacing.

Looking over at the lady on the bench
   next to us, you smile. She is
in and out of a large bag counting
   and recounting her worldly goods.

A man shuffles out into the garden
   and comes over to her.
They argue and he goes back inside,
   repeating this many times.

You say, "That's her boy friend.
   They argue all the time, but
need each other. And who am I
   to talk about them?" recognizing
in them your sometime self.

But today, we sit together again,
   our earlier selves,
discussing politics, philosophy, family,
   poetry and the state of the world.
Your humor laced through it,
   a balm from Gilead.

*From the Negro spiritual, "There is a balm in Gilead."

Solace

in the sun
on my shoulders
in chartreuse flowers
spilling from split buds
even the freight train
rattling my horizon.
Solace
in the chevron
on the flicker's neck
in catkins furred in gold
and I can let go
my son
on the Florida bay
his disdainful eye
no more vivid
than cold blue patches
on the jay.
He smokes his third cigarette
of the morning.
Elm glow! willow glow! –
and I can leave him
in his makeshift dinghy
wide feet relaxed
in flip-flops
dark hairs sprouting
from his toes.

Myrna Patterson

Mother's Day, no children

After my surgery, before answers, dozens of deep purple tulips
arise from winter's hard brown crust, nodding regally to daffodils
and grape hyacinths, forming a circle around me as I lie in the sun.

This is no small event, my friends' prayers floating to me
from everywhere and me wondering if my children will
ever see me again or if I'll melt into pure consciousness.

Truth is, I am alive and well, the finches are squabbling with
the mourning doves over black seed. I watch spring sun
pierce pink azalea buds and splash onto thick red bricks.

Truth is, my kids are living their lives, all grown.
I have only to sit, to walk, to lie down, to eat
fresh strawberries, breathe, love, and let go,

The Third Noble Truth: the way it is, no suffering.

Pearl Garrett Crayton

Potentially Fatal Toes

Please, please, please, please, please
don't step on my daughter's toes!
You might not be strong enough to survive,
and I might be too old to endure watching
what she might do to you –
cut down to size,
scratch your eyes out,
pull out your hair,
go for your jugular vein,
flay you skinless,
trample you in the dust.
I've seen cancers cause less misery.
So please, please, please
walk carefully into her presence,
for her toes extend from here to yonder,
protecting her honor, her ideas,
her misconceptions, her church,
her philosophy of life, her unfounded suspicions,
her home, her husband, her country,
her investments, her company, her inadequacies,
her sorority, her family, her friends,
her aspirations, her prejudices,
gigantic toes that very few
ever manage to avoid.
Please, please don't risk wasting time
admiring my daughter's pretty face or her shapely body.
Ignore her intelligence and her brilliant discourse,
and concentrate every moment of your time,
every iota of your intelligence,
every ampere of your energy
on avoiding the potentially fatal error
of stepping on her toes.

Five for Lunch

My friend the stranger wears the pinched look
of fresh sorrow.
Her brother in Ireland died last month, leaving
a bewildered wife, four kids and no insurance.

She doesn't want to be here, that much is clear –
her eyes look over our heads to something
beyond the café's stained glass windows,
her pursed lips trembling ever so slightly.

But this moment is not for giving loss its due,
and the rest of us exclaim over our pasta and wine,
our voices rising like a chorus of cicadas.

We break in on each other in a farce of gaiety,
smiling, raising our forks like lances in the
afternoon light.

We tell half-finished stories, laugh or groan on cue,
talk about a recent exhibit, the one with Trotsky and
Rivera, but mostly Frida Kahlo (who loved and suffered
so extravagantly) the way I would like to but only
dream about.

I think suddenly of my son, a middle-aged stranger,
of my daughters who can barely keep their own sorrows
at rapier's end...
Nevertheless.

I want to tell my bereft friend, look!
We have to learn to cut our losses like you cut bait.
But suddenly ashamed, I pass the bread to her waiting
hands, avoid her grieving eyes.

Jocasta Interviewed in Hell

Well, naturally I blamed myself – blamed myself for giving up my baby – we all do, you know, even those who say we don't. Being queen of Thebes was no compensation, though Laius insisted it would be. I don't say he made me do it, though being king he made me understand he could have. Laius was always a bully anyway, and a bit dull, as many bullies are. If he thought he could confound the oracle, if he really believed he could defeat the old ones, why did I have to make that choice? Why did I have to send my child away?

Later I understood how great his fear had been. But when we argued, while we argued, I had no idea. I was so young then, still crying over my loose belly, still soaked in milk – I had set down my own power, and he was the king. He said, Send the child away; turn it out. And I did. I did what he asked.

And so the queen of Corinth raised my son. Her servants and tutors grew him into a strong one who left home on a tide of fear, fearfilled love for his parents – love for his *parents*! But then, like any animal with instinct for the blood of its birth, he came back to be my lover, my mysterious suitor, the supposed savior of my city.

You people always ask why I didn't recognize him, but have you ever seen a newborn? Or even a beloved six month infant? Do you think I have the gift, the eye of the Graiae? Do you? Can you look at such children and imagine who they'll be at 18, standing in front of you? I think not. When you look down at them in their baskets, wrapped in soft cloth, when they root for the nipple under your gown, pursing their tiny budlipped mouths toward the smell of you, their eyes still fogged, still changing? How could I have *recognized* him?

The Teachings

of my grandmother
who at over eighty
went west from West Acton,
to see a long lost son named
Archie – by Greyhound, my
other uncle, Hap, got the *Globe*
to photograph her, and us –
came back from Riverside, California,
where Archie was – he'd left
at eighteen – and he'd tried,
she told us, to teach her
religion, "at her age" – "as
much a fool as ever" – and
she never spoke of him again.

Listen

– for Rebecca

Having lost you, I attract substitutes.
The student poets visit, think me wise,
Think me generous, confide in me.
Earnestly they sit in my office
Showing me their stigmata
Under the Judy Chicago poster
Of her half-opened writhing-petalled
Clitoris that appears to wheel
Slowly clockwise when you gaze at it,
And I sympathize. Then they try on their ambitions
Like stiff new hiking boots, and I laugh
And approve, telling them where to climb.
They bring me tiny plastic bags
Of healthy seeds and nuts, they bring me wine,
We huddle by the electric heater
When it is snowing,
We watch the sparrows dash
And when they leave we hug.

Oh silly mother, I can hear you mock.
Listen, loveliest, I am not unaware
This is as it must be.
Do daughters mock their mother? Is Paris
A city? Do your pouring hormones
Cause you to do the slam
And other Dionysiac dances,
And did not even Sappho tear her hair
And act undignified, when the maiden
She wanted, the girl with the soft lips,
The one who could dance,
Deserted her?

Alicia Ostriker

Do I suffer? Of course I do,
I am supposed to, but listen, loveliest.
I want to be a shrub, you a tree.
I hum inaudibly and want you
To sing arias. I want to lie down
At the foot of your mountain
And rub the two dimes in my pocket
Together, while you dispense treasure
To the needy. I want the gods
Who have eluded me
All my life, or whom I have eluded,
To invite you regularly
To their lunches and jazz recitals.
Moreover I wish to stand on the dock
All by myself waving a handkerchief,
And you to be the flagship
Sailing from the midnight harbor,
A blue moon leading you outward,
So huge, so public, so disappearing –

I beg and beg, loveliest, I can't
Seem to help myself,
While you quiver and pull
Back, and try to hide, try to be
Invisible, like a sensitive
Irritated sea animal
Caught in a tide pool, caught
Under my hand, can I
Cut off my hand for you,
Cut off my life.

Lowater Bridge

Next to a copse of redbud
that shelters this spot from the freeway,
I lean against trunks the grey of elephants,
blink away the fog. Your words
reverberate inside my skull, muffling
the racket of cars to the on-ramps
that could be our collisions with each other.

I stare at the water's swirl, the routes
from my eyes to my brain opening and closing
like fish mouths. You would have your words
drop at my feet, stay there like stones.
But I rub them in my fingers,
break them apart, hold up fragments
to the light. Find versions of myself
like grit trapped in agate.

I barely know where the sun is
in the skim-milk sky, I think
it's my own soul paling. Echoes
crest, then break, crest and break,
pulses of a distant truck on the highway.

This hold we have on one another.

When I go back to the house
we will be on guard, we will behave
well: recoil, as the French say,
the better to spring ahead.

Harmonies for the Alienation of My Daughter

I wish I could put her in the birdhouse.
Evicted from her rented room,
she pushes a wheelchair through rain
when only prowl cars can watch her.
I am tossing, it is no dream
she pushes her belongings through night rain
to someplace wet and cold she will belong.
How have I let this happen?
I wish I could put her in the birdhouse.

Some days she bikes to work,
washes the unmovable man in bed,
cleans the quadriplegic quarterback's
cave and then his parrot's cage,
fastens baby's breath in the paralyzed
woman's hair for the opera.
Some days she comes home fired, lies
down in earphones on the floor,
and cannot cry.

If she is moth-crazy (nice Navaho for mad),
she makes reparations to the moths
by opening the night door to her light.
Then she goes up on the roof,
says it is covered with little white rocks
and mushrooms. Says: "It is so silent."
Says: "The stars are writing a bit
like you but not keeping a file on me
like you." Says: "Mother –

Mother's crazy too."

A Present I Didn't Know I Wanted

Let's get back to San Francisco, heedless
as rabbits rampaging after food and happiness
in the wet air, let's feed the indiscriminate hunger
of mother and daughters, let's go back
through the boutiques of Berkeley, where I could buy you
black velvet again, because of your look, because
you look good in past eras, because the present squeezes
you. We've covered almost everything,
I've told you everything and you've told me
something. What was it you couldn't swallow,
I'd asked tactlessly, so you left out the rest, and for years
San Francisco was off limits. Last week you brought her back,
an act waiting in the wings, that 19th century hussy
anxious to revive her lanterns, her smoke, her seductive
edgy illusion of freedom. No more talking,
all has been said. I've told you why childhood hurts,
that bruises are mothers and fathers who miss the point
on alternate days, that no life will ever be done in time.
We suspected it anyway when we both stopped crying
for awhile. We stopped telling jokes.
Our throats became damaged from the broken vocabulary.
We invented a dialect full of chilliness and blind spots
like the misty mid valleys of California where cars pile up
soundlessly because tules shroud the true hazards until it is
too late. You drove down to see me scared
of collisions, losing time here and there, stopping
for lunch rather than reflection, but coming back to your
cousins and nephews, inevitable sibling lapses,
seeing the suitcase I've saved full of old visas and pictures,
your father's dead uncles whose names I've forgotten,
the smell of tobacco, the tangle and pull
of the family wiring, you say let's go back to San Francisco
where we shopped like actresses and spent like mistresses
and laughed like sisters. I'd love that. Thank you for asking.

The Blessing

for Ashley

I.

Daughter-my-mother
you have observed my worst.
Holding me together at your expense
has made you burn cool.

So did I in childhood:
nursed her old hurts and doubts,
myself made cool to shallowness.
She grew out as I grew in.
At midpoint, our furies met.

My mother's dust has rested
for fifteen years
in the front hall closet
because we couldn't bear to bury it.
Her dust-lined, dust-coated urn
squats among the size-eleven overshoes.
My father, who never forgets
his overshoes,
has forgotten that.

Hysterical-tongued daughter
of a dead marriage,
you shed hot tears in the bed
of that benign old woman
whose fierce joy you were:
tantrums in her closet
taking upon yourself the guilt
the split parents never felt.

Carolyn Kizer

Child and old woman
soothing each other,
sharing the same face
in a span of seventy years,
the same mother wit.

II.

I must go home, says my father,
his mind straying:
*this is a hard time
for your mother.* But she's been dead
these fifteen years.
Daughter and daughter, we sit
on either side.
Whose? Which? He's not sure.
After long silence,
don't press me, he says.

Mother, hysterical-tongued,
age and grace burned away
your excesses, left
that lavender-sweet child
who turned up the thermostat
on her electric blanket, folded
her hands on her breast.
You had dreamed death
as a silver prince:
like marrying Nehru, you said.

Dearest, does your dust hum
in the front hall closet –
this is a hard time for me –
among umbrella points,
the canes, and overshoes
of that cold climate?

Each week she denies it,
my blithe mother
in that green, cloud-free landscape
where we whisper our dream-secrets
to each other.

III.

Daughter, you lived through
my difficult affairs
as I tried to console
your burnt-out childhood.
We coped with our fathers,
compared notes
on the old one and the cold one,
learned to moderate our hates.
Risible in suffering,
we grew up together.

Mother-my-daughter
I have been blessed
on both sides of my life.
Forgive me if sometimes
like my fading father
I see you as one.

Not that I confuse
your two identities
as he does, taking off
or putting on his overshoes,
but my own role:

I lean on the bosom
of that double mother,
the ghost by night, the girl by day;
I between my
two mild furies,
alone but comforted.

And I will whisper blithely
in your dreams
when you are as old as I,
my hard time over.
Meanwhile, keep warm
your love, your bed,
and your wise heart and head,
my good daughter.

Betty Buchsbaum

Why We Missed Our Flight

If our husbands had pressed us
　　to say what we were talking about

that we failed to hear our boarding call,
　　I might have stammered out details

of the funeral we'd gone to.
　　But that wouldn't have told the story.

As we sat in that noisy airport,
　　mother and daughter huddled

in a makeshift privacy,
　　all we said about the sadness

in that house, about the child
　　who asked at graveside if Pop was going

to sit up in his box and speak
　　before he got planted in that hole,

all that we poured out, wanting to grab
　　whatever time we had

to catch up on your children, our writing,
　　my Red Sea swim with dolphins,

all our words, like small fish darting
　　on the ocean's surface,

turned on a deeper current –
　　our talking   and listening

a warm, delicious tangle
    like suckling each other –

oh somewhere I heard a voice
    announce *last call to...*

heard you come up for air,
    they calling us?

heard me protest *no, no, it can't*
    be time!...felt us both sink back,

our coupled voices muffling
    all summons for departure.

Marie Ponsot

Between

For my daughter

Composed in a shine of laughing, Monique brings in sacks
of groceries, unloads them, straightens, and stretches her back.

The child was a girl, the girl is a woman; the shift
is subtle and absolute, worn like a gift.

The woman, once girl once child, now is deft in her ease,
is door to the forum, is cutter of keys.

In space that her torque and lift have prefigured and set free
between her mother and her child the woman stands
having emptied her hands.

Linda Pastan

Practicing

My son is practicing the piano.
He is a man now, not the boy
whose lessons I once sat through,
whose reluctant practicing
I demanded – part of the obligation
I felt to the growth
and composition of a child.

Upstairs my grandchildren are sleeping,
though they complained earlier of the music
which rises like smoke up through the floorboards,
coloring the fabric of their dreams.
On the porch my husband watches the garden fade
into summer twilight, flower by flower;
it must be a little like listening to the fading

diminuendo notes of Mozart.
But here where the dining room table
has been pushed aside to make room
for this second or third-hand upright,
my son is playing the kind of music
it took him all these years,
and sons of his own, to want to make.

Reprise

Thirty years later she takes up the violin again
learning in three days more than she did in three months
when she was eight then she adds pieces incrementally
as if to propel herself past that year she stalled
unheard, inept, not yet intoxicated enough. This time
the wrong notes do not cause me pain, though I notice
she plays the same song on which her lessons ended.
It's enough she has taken the interim years down deep
beneath my carelessness. I see her in her child, on whom
I dote with ease; my daughter gives me that latitude but
plants herself between us, holding the bow just so, more
diligence now in her hands, more patience in her shoulders,
teaching us both how to grow serious passion at every age.
We have spent years speaking of reconciliation while her
six year old daughter speaks to me of the books she reads.
These are not sentimental second chances, they are
hard stand-up intentions, a steady practice that keeps my
back from bending, my bones from breaking.

Girl Children

Lena gave birth to Marion and Marion gave birth to Nancy
and Nancy gave birth to Lise and Batia
and Lise gave birth to Lucy and Batia gave birth to Ruby

Unto the Generations

Remember: Lise's felt Santa,
its beard a comic parenthesis.

Marion's words to comfort
the confusions of 11-year-old Nancy,
illustrated by a pen-and-ink sketch:
See how the walls are at 90 degree angles to the floor and ceiling.
If they were lesser or greater, the room would be out of perspective.
That's how it is in life. You try to keep things in proportion
to one another and to the whole.

Think about the impulse to say sorry to a chair.

Recall Sappho's tender fragment:
I have a lovely little girl who looks
like golden flowers, cherished Kleis,
whom I would not exchange for all
of Lydia...

...Unto the generations...unto...

Big Sister Marion

Four younger ones
skated on Lake Onondaga, played stickball
in the elm-lined street, were admonished
at the dining room table, "Settle down."

Even before Papa died,
it was my job to help Mama,
wring out the heavy wash, hang it
crisscross in the back yard; bones were
cheap at the butcher on Salinas St.
I set them to boil, sliced onions,
carrots and potatoes into the big soup pot.
Healer of small hurts,
averter of mundane disasters, I read
Sense and Sensibility, The Scarlet Pimpernel,
dreamed a city of lights,
symphonies and showtunes,
a separate self.

Nancy, Age 6

I couldn't learn to add
or subtract 2-digit numbers.
Carrying over and taking away
were continuity and loss.
To get an answer (not a solution)
you couldn't guess what might
be saved, what might be discounted.
Oneness was all I had.

Marion. A Short Life

I like to think I was a thoroughly modern woman. I married the
waiter from summer camp. He went to law school; I dressed with
flair, but I was no mere decoration. I researched décor at the antique
company library on Fifth Avenue – rows of books on Chippendale,
medieval armor, textiles, an illuminated icon in a niche near the door.

There are two parts to a woman's life difficult to reconcile. We moved to the country, close to the capitol. He drafted laws, drank with politicians. I planted hollyhocks under my daughter's bedroom window, papered the living room walls with celadon damask, got the old stone fireplace working. Being a homemaker wasn't enough; I did it as a girl. My husband's pride wouldn't let me work. His father had abandoned the family. I left him, went back to my old job.

> I needed just one man;
> when I found him
> he already had a wife, a debt
> that could be repaid only
> by keeping things
> as they were.
> Our love bloomed, though we had
> to reach across a continent
> to tend it, until I left everything
> (except my child) to be with him.

With divorce money from the farmhouse I bought a girls' dress factory, designed broadcloth and organdy, dotted swiss and dimity, sizes 1-6x. I copied Pinkie's dress in Sir Thomas Lawrence's painting, soft flowing white folds with a wide satin sash.

They came to my hospital bed every evening. Five months.

> "What will happen to me?" Nancy asks.
> "You'll be able to take care of youself.
> I never meant to leave you so soon."
> She puts her arms around me. I'm all bones.
> "On the blank wall opposite," I tell her,
> "I see an antique tapestry,
> 'Mille Fleurs' – against a pale green background,
> countless tiny dark flowers."

Nancy Kassell

Nancy. A Short Childhood

Evenings, anger mounted the pine staircase and invaded the
dark of my bedroom. Mama gained 30 pounds, took me to her
mother's, then to Mexico, where I learned the difference between
Madre and *mamacita* and rescued stray cats.

Twenty minutes before the train pulled into San Francisco, she
told me, "A man will be meeting us." He was portly, balding, had
a little moustache. "Come with me to the Casbah!" he said to me in
his best Charles Boyer voice on the way to his car. *No idea how to
talk to a child*, I thought scornfully, but what I meant was: *Why can't
I have her to myself?*

I read the English poets –

> *Tell me where is fancy bred,*
> *Or in the heart or in the head?*
> *How begot, how nourished?*
> *Reply, reply.*

Austen and Stendhal, *True Detective* and *True Romance*. They
took day trips to Santa Rosa, Sonoma. In the back seat I puzzled
over the confinements of women and children.

His wife stood at the top of the dark stairs, her long gray braid
wrapped around her head. She opened her arms: "I'm so sorry
about your mother. She made him a much kinder man." *Not to me*,
I wanted to say. But what I meant was, *Neither of us wanted to share her.*

First Born, to very young parents, a perfect girl child,
    Lise, blond as the sun, serene as a rosebud.

Nancy Kassell

Daughter: I grew up thinking you didn't like me.

Mother: *I was a rebel. Determined not to choose between thinking, studying, writing and motherhood.*

Daughter: Didn't you see what was happening?

Mother: *Your father was present and not present, a wanderer by nature. He took you from me, made you his playmate. He transfigured me into a dark spirit of duty and striving.*

Daughter: Why didn't you fight for me?

Mother: *I went underground; spoke too little and too softly. There was no light, there were no guides: my mother, grandmother, aunt all dead. I thought anger was death. I was wrong. Silence is.*

Nancy Advises Her Grown Daughters

    Once and for long years, marriage was
    a ritual sacrifice: a woman's self
    torn apart like flesh and bone, scattered
    across the terrain of her girlhood–
    to be reassembled
    as usage and masquerade.

    Become the artist of yourself.

    The Furies of Fragmentation will pursue you,
    hungry to feed on the bonds of love:
    traffic jams on the freeway, fevers and tantrums,
    deadlines, sleep deprivation, errant
    socks, sibling rivalry, the milk

Nancy Kassell

you forgot to pick up. Keep in mind Alcestis
as antimodel; in a family, everyone makes
sacrifices, none life-threatening.

Mother of the Bride

I step onto the bed and open the zipper
which wends its way down the bodice
to the skirt, reach up under the lining
and take first one, then the other shoulder
from the hanger. She stands in gold ballet
slippers, nude push-up bra, crinoline slip,
looking up at me.

                    I raise the dress
over her head and let the fluid silk
slide over her body as once,
anointed with birth waters,
she slid out of mine.

Ruby

Ten months old, already autonomous:
She stands up, walks and does laps –
the kitchen island, the dining room,
the living room. Again.
When you read to her,
she has to read back to you,
though she has almost no words yet.

Lucy

I take her into my arms:
forty-five minutes old.
Her face is changeful as light
on water. She holds
my eyes with hers.
Who are you?
Who am I?

Unto the Generations

Daughters, we birth you
into a world we will remake.
First we burn the tanglewood.
Then you teach us
the language
of transformation.

The Children

Not you, but what they made of you
is what they've taken
to shape their lives.

Not you, but some monster
who walked across a field in a golden sweater
while they trailed behind.

Not you, but a pair of eyes,
a wet flash of anger,
or some approving smile for some small thing they did.

You teasing or laughing,
skipping stones across some placid river,
back there in their minds.

Not you, but something in some other world
of their own making,
looking down on them – or praising

what they can't praise themselves.
You frozen in time,
the you that is not you forever theirs.

Lisel Mueller

Bedtime Story

The moon lies on the river
like a drop of oil.
The children come to the banks to be healed
of their wounds and bruises.
The fathers who gave them their wounds and bruises
come to be healed of their rage.
The mothers grow lovely; their faces soften,
the birds in their throats awake.
They all stand hand in hand
and the trees around them,
forever on the verge
of becoming one of them,
stop shuddering and speak their first word.

But that is not the beginning.
It is the end of the story,
and before we come to the end,
the mothers and fathers and children
must find their way to the river,
separately, with no one to guide them.
That is the long, pitiless part,
and it will scare you.

David Ignatow

For My Daughter

1.
I was never so happy
as when you were born.
Everything
that did not conform
to your laughter
I let go.
In your delight
I was that child.

Work became a fable
of a man surviving
for your sustenance.
I worked as a religion
of which you were the sign,
I an acolyte
in my faith in you.

2.
My daughter, we will not meet
often from now on, separated
by distance and time,
but you are close to me.

At my age our next meeting
may be our last. I'm alive
to say so.

I cared, my thought of you,
your life assured because you love.

3.
My daughter's first gray hairs
remind me of the time
I looked on mine with curiosity
at forty, her age exactly.
She is my daughter, no doubt.

We both are traveling
in the same direction
together in our separate graves.

Alice Ryerson Hayes

Unnaming as a Preparation for Winter

for Susan Moon

See the old woman sitting on a park bench?
The park lies around her, dismantling itself for winter.
They are both preparing to be minimalists.
The grass is conserving its energy, browning out.
The trees are casting off their spare parts
in disorganized piles.
The no longer flourishing flowers
are being tidied away by the park keepers.
The crackable fountains are empty and dry.

The old woman is also dismantling herself.
Her pinkness is fading.
She is casting off hair and extra skin.
She grows dry and crackly like a potato chip,
preserves herself like a salt fish.
As the storage space inside her
shrinks smaller and tighter
she is casting out names.

Still, you mustn't worry.
She is saving enough space to keep you in:
your color and sound, your essential shape,
the way it feels when a sandwich goes
from your hand into hers, your warm kitchen,
how good it felt to have you in her womb.

She is cleaning out names to make room
for all this. So that even if your name
should be spilled out with the others,
you will be packed away intact.

Autumn in the Yard We Planted

Whoever said that I should count on mind?
Think it through, think it up – now that I know so much,
what's left to think is the unthinkable.

And the will has grown too tired to stamp its foot.
It sings a vapid song, it dithers and mopes,
it takes its basket to the marketplace,
like a schoolgirl in her best dress, and watches
others ask outright for what they want –
how do they know what they want? – and haul it away,
the sweet, the dull, the useless and the dear.

A maudlin, whimpering song: in which I lament
my own children, scything their separate paths
into the field, one with steady strokes,
one in a rage. We taught them that. And,
not to look back: at the apple tree, first
to shatter its petals onto the clipped grass,
or the slovenly heads of the russet peonies,

or even that late-to-arrive pastel, all stalk
with a few staggered blossoms, meadow rue –
though surely they could see it from where they are.

One of the Softer Sorrows of Age

I asked
did this happen before you moved to New York or
just after you rented the house   the one that
was once a shed   it did look nice finally   or
was it afterwards   when you found that great old farmhouse
way out of the village on the dirt road   when was it...

She answered
why do you talk like that   everybody is forgetful
what are you trying to prove

my dear girl   I AM growing old

oh ma   ma...

Judith W. Steinbergh

Writing My Will

About the matter of my body once I've died –
The spirit's always been of most concern.
I just don't know my children, you decide.

Maybe I'll rest on the rural hill beside
my mother, the warm earth, her freckled arms
about the matter of my body. Once I've died

I won't much care. After you've mourned and cried,
sing the songs I wrote and say the poems
I used to know. My children, you decide

which of the many places that I've loved
my ashes might be scattered if I burn.
It's just a matter of the body. Once I've died

if the season's right, I'll probably reside
at Kezar Lake or ledgy Annisquam;
I just don't know, my children. You decide

what will ease your pain. I'm satisfied
to help the lettuce and the raspberries return
over the matter of my body. Once I've died
I just won't know, my children. You decide.

Linda Pastan

Sometimes

from the periphery
of the family
where I sit watching
my children and
my children's children
in all their bright
cacophony,

I seem to leave
my body –
plump effigy
of a woman, upright
on a chair –
and as I float
willingly away

toward the chill
silence of my own future,
their voices break
into the syllables
of strangers, to whom
with this real hand
I wave goodbye.

38 years later

Where did that unwanted baby
go? Tony was born, and we went
on to love and hate each other
like twins. But some place lodged in my psyche
like a splinter is the one
whose body he occupied
for a second.
When the doctor said, "It's too late
for an abortion.
It happens to lots of girls,"
I could see a big balloon open before me,
like a gray heart I could have stepped
into. It scared me and I stopped
my little heart from going.
Then I went out in my little skirt, an
attractive slim woman
who later was told by a Weight Watcher's counselor,
"What a waste of womanhood!"
because I wouldn't lose
that ten extra pounds.
I know how I turned out as a mother.
I know how Tony turned out as a man.
Not perfect, but pretty good.
But if all moments are immortal,
I wonder how that baby I didn't want
turned out? And what about the mother
I didn't want to be?

Time, Place, and Parenthood

Here we are, my son, aliens in this place
That seems so remote from our origin among
The superb slopes and deep valleys of the Green
Mountains, only a day's drive to the east.
Most people nowadays think aliens
Must come from Mars, and indeed sometimes
I feel remarkably Martian, so apparent
Are even the little distinctions of time and place
To me in my old age. And sometimes also
You now in your maturity of body and mind,
Your handsome strength, seem so distinct from
The four-year-old boy who rode beside me
In our pickup over the mountains, or the six-
Year-old who built the hut under the roots
Of the half-washed-out hemlock by the brook,
That I can recall you only as in a faded
Photograph from another country. But no,
It isn't true, not for more than an instant. I still
Remember you clinging in my arms as we ran
Down the tilt of Marshall's pasture, or holding
My hand as we entered the little post office
In our old town, so loving, so loyal. In these,
My son, you have been constant; almost four
Decades later you are the same. My son –
My Bo, my David – my man now in this world –
Accept these words that can never say enough.

Credits

Hayden Carruth. "Pittsburgh" from *Scrambled Eggs & Whiskey: Poems 1991-1995*. Copyright ©1996 by Hayden Carruth and "Time, Place, and Parenthood" from *Doctor Jazz*. Copyright ©2001 by Hayden Carruth. Reprinted by permission of Copper Canyon Press, P.O. Box 271, Port Townsend, WA 98368-0271.

Raymond Carver. "To my Daughter" and "On an Old Photograph of My Son" from *All of Us: The Collected Poems* by Raymond Carver, copyright ©1996 by Tess Gallagher. Introduction copyright ©1996 by Tess Gallagher. Editor's preface, commentary and notes copyright ©1996 by William L. Stull. Used by permission of Alfred A. Knopf, a division of Random House, Inc.

Elizabeth Claman. "The Queens of Ice Cream" by Elizabeth Claman was first published in *Passionate Lives*, Queen of Swords Press, 1998.

Robert Creeley. "The Teachings" by Robert Creeley from *Collected Poems of Robert Creeley. 1945-75*, ©1983. Reprinted by permission of The Regents of the University of California.

Cortney Davis. "How I Imagine It" is reprinted from *Details of Flesh* by Cortney Davis, ©1997, by permission of the publisher, Calyx Books.

Marilyn Hacker. "Grief" from *Squares and Courtyards* by Marilyn Hacker. Copyright ©2000 by Marilyn Hacker. Used by permission of W.W. Norton & Company, Inc.

Alice Ryerson Hayes. "Unnaming as a Preparation for Winter" and "Imagining Water" by Alice Ryerson Hayes were first published in *Journal of the Lake: Excerpts from a Seventieth Year*, Open Books, 1997.

David Ignatow. "For my Daughter" from *Living is What I Wanted: Last Poems*. Copyright ©1999 by Yaedi Ignatow. Reprinted with the permission of BOA Editions, Ltd.

Carolyn Kizer. "The Blessing" from *Cool, Calm, and Collected: Poems 1960-2000*. Copyright ©2001 by Carolyn Kizer. Reprinted by permission of Copper Canyon Press, P.O. Box 271, Port Townsend, WA 98368-0271.

Penelope Scambly Schott. "Hours After the Phone Call" by Penelope Scambly Schott was first published in *Passager*.

Myra Shapiro. "Rise and Shine" was first published in *Connecticut River Review*, Summer 2002.

Judith Steinbergh. "Writing My Will" by Judith W. Steinbergh was first published in *Writing My Will*, Talking Stone Press, Boston, 2002.

Ruth Stone. "The Ways of Daughters" from *Ordinary Words* by Ruth Stone. Copyright ©1999 by Ruth Stone. Reprinted by permission of Paris Press.

Betsy Thorne. "The Moment" was published in a slightly different form and titled "A Momentous Occasion" in *Lonzie's Fried Chicken*.

Ellen Bryant Voigt. "Autumn in the Yard We Planted," from *Shadow of Heaven* by Ellen Bryant Voigt. Copyright ©2002 by Ellen Bryant Voigt. Used by permission of W.W. Norton & Company, Inc.

Contributors

Dick Allen's latest poetry book, his seventh, is *The Day Before: New Poems* (Sarabande Books, 2003). He has received poetry writing grants from the NEA and Ingram Merrill Foundations and numerous national prizes for poetry. His poems have appeared in *The Best American Poetry*, *Atlantic Monthly*, and *Poetry*, among other journals.

Judith Arcana's writing has appeared in many journals, including *Prairie Schooner* and *Nimrod*. Among her prose works is *Grace Paley's Life Stories, A Literary Biography*. She has received a variety of awards, grants and residencies.

Jill Breckenridge won The Bluestem Award in 1990 for her book of poems *How To Be Lucky*. *Civil Blood*, a sequence of poetry and prose about the Civil War period, was published by Milkweed Editions. The book was nominated for a National Book Critics' Circle Award and the American Library Association's Notable Books of 1986.

Betty Buchsbaum, Professor Emeritus at Mass. College of Art, returned to writing poems in the past decade. Her poems have been published in journals that include *Spoon River Review, Peregrine, Kalliope* and *Lilith*. She has given readings in the Boston area. Her first collection will be published in 2004 by Chicory Blue Press.

Hayden Carruth has published twenty-three books of poetry, including *Scrambled Eggs & Whiskey*, which won the National Book Award, and *Collected Shorter Poems*, which won the National Book Critics Circle Award. *Doctor Jazz* was published in 2001.

Raymond Carver's six volumes of poetry are gathered in *All of Us, The Collected Poems* (Knopf, 1998).

Elizabeth Claman's poetry and fiction have appeared in *River Styx, Alaska Quarterly Review* and other journals and anthologies. She was Editor-in-Chief of Queen of Swords Press and Associate Editor of *Northwest Review* and *Five Fingers Review*.

Michele Cooper is widely published in literary magazines and is winner of several poetry prizes. She is the author of two books, founding editor of the *Newport Review* and of a chapbook series, *Premier Poets.*

Pearl Garrett Crayton's work has appeared in anthologies and journals, including *Kente Cloth, The Crimson Edge: Older Women Writing, Volume Two, Rites of Passage: Stories About Growing Up by Black Writers Around the World.* Her work has received awards, including the Frances Shaw Fellowship from Ragdale Foundation.

Robert Creeley's poetry is gathered most recently in *The Collected Poems 1945-1975* (Berkeley, CA, 1982) and *Selected Poems 1945-90* (London and New York, 1991). He founded *The Black Mountain Review.*

Cortney Davis's most recent book is *I Knew a Woman* (Ballantine), a memoir about her work in women's health care. She is also author of the poetry collection, *Details of Flesh* (Calyx) and co-editor of two anthologies of poetry and prose by nurses, *Between the Heartbeats* and *Intensive Care* (University of Iowa Press). She is recipient of an NEA Poetry Fellowship.

Deborah DeNicola edited the anthology *Orpheus & Company: Contemporary Poems on Greek Mythology* (The University Press of New England). She is the author of *Where Divinity Begins* (Alice James Press) and two chapbooks. She has received awards for her poetry.

Toi Derricotte's two most recent books are *Tender,* which won the 1998 Paterson Poetry Prize, and *The Black Notebooks,* a literary memoir that was a *New York Times* Notable Book.

Sheila Gardiner has been writing poetry since second grade, but has been able to focus her energies on it only since retirement. She was winner of the Frances Shaw Fellowship for women who made a commitment to writing later in life. Several of her poems have been featured on the Chicory Blue Press website.

Kinereth Gensler has three books of poetry with Alice James Books. The latest, *Journey Fruit,* includes a memoir. She is co-author of *The Poetry Connection: An Anthology of Contemporary Poems with Ideas to Stimulate Children's Writing.* She has taught in the Radcliffe Seminars for many years.

Diane Gregory has practiced psychoanalysis for twenty-six years. She began to write poetry six years ago. She has given poetry readings in New York City. This is her first publication.

Marilyn Hacker is the author of nine books, including *Winter Numbers* (W.W. Norton) which received the Lenore Marshall Prize of the Academy of American Poets and *The Nation* magazine, and a Lambda Literary Award. Her *Selected Poems* received the Poets' Prize in 1996. A new collection, *Desesperanto*, will be published by W.W. Norton in the spring of 2003.

Alice Ryerson Hayes has published poems in many journals, including *Spoon River Poetry Review, Women's Review of Books, Prairie Schooner* and *Primavera*. She has published four books of poetry, most recently, *Journal of the Lake, Excerpts from a Seventieth Year* (Open Books).

David Ignatow is the author of eighteen volumes of poetry. Among other awards, he received the Bollingen Prize, two Guggenheim Fellowships, and an award from the National Institute of Arts and Letters "for a lifetime of creative effort." His last book of poems is *Living is What I Wanted, Last Poems*.

Nancy Kassell has published poetry in *Spoon River Poetry Review, Southern Poetry Review, Feminist Review* and *Salamander*, as well as in two anthologies. Author of two librettos for opera, she has also published a nonfiction book, *The Pythia on Ellis Island, Rethinking the Greco-Roman Legacy in America*.

Carolyn Kizer's most recent book, *Cool, Calm & Collected*, gathers new poems together with selections from previous volumes. She received the Pulitzer Prize in poetry in 1984 for her collection *Yin* and the 1988 Theodore Roethke Award.

Maxine Kumin has published twelve volumes of poetry. Her *Selected Poems: 1960-1990* was a *New York Times* Notable Book of the Year. She was awarded the Pulitzer Prize for poetry in 1973 and in recent years has won the Ruth Lilly Prize and the Robert Frost Contemporary American Award.

Carrie Allen McCray (b. 1913, Lynchburg Virginia) was a social worker and college teacher. Her chapbook, *Piece of Time*, was published in 1993 by Chicory Blue Press. The story of her mother, *Freedom's Child*, was published in 1998 by Algonquin. She has completed a narrative poem, "Ota's Song," about the pygmy who lived in her home when she was a child.

Sandra McPherson's most recent book is *A Visit to Civilization*. Her other poetry collections include *Edge Effect: Trails and Portrayals, The Spaces Between Birds*, and *The God of Indeterminacy*. Her book, *The Year of Our Birth*, was a finalist for the National Book Award in 1978.

Lisel Mueller is author of *Alive Together: New and Selected Poems*, winner of the Pulitzer Prize for poetry in 1996, and of several other award-winning volumes of poems, including *Waving from Shore*, awarded the 1990 Carl Sandburg Prize.

Monica Ochtrup is author of two books of poetry, *What I Cannot Say/ I Will Say* and *Pieces from the Long Afternoon*, both from New Rivers Press. She is recipient of a Loft-McKnight Award of Distinction in Poetry.

Carole Simmons Oles is author of five collections of poems, most recently *Sympathetic Systems*. Her poems appear in *American Poetry Review, Kenyon Review* and *Prairie Schooner*, among other periodicals. She has received the Clator and Lake Prizes from the Poetry Society of America.

Alicia Ostriker is the author of ten volumes of poetry, the most recent of which is *the volcano sequence*. Her work has been finalist twice for the National Book Award, won the William Carlos Williams Award of the Poetry Society of America, the Paterson Poetry Award and the San Francisco State Poetry Center Award.

Grace Paley is author of *Begin Again, Collected Poems*. In 1994, her *Collected Stories* was a finalist for the National Book Award.

Linda Pastan's *Carnival Evening: New and Selected Poems 1968-1998* was finalist for the National Book Award. Recent books include *Heroes in Disguise* and *An Early Afterlife*.

Myrna Patterson's poems have been published in *Martha Vineyard Gazette, Squaw Valley Review, Insight Magazine* and are forthcoming in the anthology, *Martha's Vineyard: A Collection.* She was a Massachusetts Cultural Council Writer-in-Residence from 1995-2000.

Greta Phinney, who wrote songs and poems as a child, for the joy of it, returned to writing in her fifties. Her poems grow out of journal entries, daydreaming, meditation. This is her second publication.

Marie Ponsot's *The Bird Catcher* won the National Book Critics Circle Award for Poetry in 1998. She has also won an NEA Creative Writing grant, the Delmore Schwartz Memorial Prize and the Shaughnessy Medal of the Modern Language Association. Her most recent collection is *Springing: New and Collected Poems.*

Jean Sands is a poet and feature writer whose work appears regularly in literary journals, magazines and newspapers. She has been nominated for a Pushcart Prize.

Pat Schneider is founder/director of Amherst Writers & Artists and AWA Press. She is author of plays, libretti and seven books including three volumes of poems, *Wake Up Laughing: A Spiritual Autobiography* and *A Continuing Passion: Writing Alone & With Others* (forthcoming from Oxford University Press).

Penelope Scambly Schott is the author of *The Perfect Mother,* a collection of poems about family, and *Penelope: The Story of the Half-Scalped Woman,* a narrative poem about an early New Jersey settler.

Myra Shapiro's book of poems, *I'll See You Thursday,* was published by Blue Sofa Press. She is currently working on a memoir, *Four Sublets: Becoming a Poet in New York.*

Elizabeth Shelley writes in her spare time, of which she has very little. She has given readings and had some of her poems published. She has completed a manuscript of poems and computer art, called *Journey: From Behind the Battered Mirror.*

Melissa Shook is a documentary photographer who has recently begun to work on poetry. This is her second publication.

Hannah Stein's books are *Earthlight*, a poetry collection and *Schools of Flying Fish*, a chapbook. Her poems have appeared widely in literary journals, including *The Antioch Review* and the *Beloit Poetry Journal.* Her poems have won national awards.

Judith W. Steinbergh's most recent poetry collections are *Writing My Will* and *A Living Anytime.* She won a Wordworks' Washington Prize and was a Bunting Institute Fellow at Radcliffe.

Ruth Stone has published twelve books. Her latest is *In the Next Galaxy.* Other recent books are *Simplicity* and *Ordinary Words*, which was the recipient of the Eric Mathieu King Award from The Academy of American Poets.

Joan Swift has published five books of poems, with *The Dark Path of Our Names* (Dragon Gate) and *The Tiger Iris* (BOA Editions, Ltd.) both winners of Washington State Governors Awards. Her *Intricate Moves, Poems about rape* was published by Chicory Blue Press in 1997. Recipient of three National Endowment for the Arts Creative Writing Fellowships, she has also won a Pushcart Prize.

Betsy Thorne is a South Carolina writer and artist. Her poems and stories have appeared in *Icarus International, Lumina* and *Lonzie's Fried Chicken.* She was best-of-issue author for poetry for *Horizons 2000*, a South Carolina Writers Workshop publication.

Madeline Tiger's poems appear in many journals and anthologies. She has published seven collections of poetry, most recently *White Owl* (Poetry New York). Her *New and Selected Poems* will appear in the spring of 2003 from Marsh Hawk Press.

Ellen Bryant Voigt, who is Vermont State Poet, has published six volumes of poetry. *Kyrie* was a Finalist for the National Book Critics Circle Award. Her most recent book is *Shadow Heaven.* Her poems appear in *The New Yorker, The Atlantic* and many literary journals. She is winner of the 2002 O.B. Hardison, Jr. Poetry Prize.

Carol Bridge Walker has had poetry and short fiction published in journals including *Southern Humanities Review, The Laurel Review, Blue Unicorn, Poetry/LA* and *The New Los Angeles Poets.*

Florence Weinberger has published two books of poems, *The Invisible Telling Its Shape* and *Breathing Like a Jew*. Her third book, *Carnal Fragrance*, is forthcoming from Red Hen Press. Her poetry has appeared widely in journals and anthologies, she has read in many venues, and her poems have won several prizes.

Victoria Wyttenberg has published in journals and anthologies, including *Poetry Northwest, Seattle Review* and *Alaska Quarterly Review*. She was awarded the Richard Hugo Prize for four poems published in *Poetry Northwest* and the Academy of American Poets Prize at the University of Washington in 1990.

Sondra Zeidenstein's poems have been published in journals and anthologies, including *Women's Review of Books, Ms. Magazine, Lilith* and *Yellow Silk*. She has published a chapbook, *Late Afternoon Woman* and a collection, *A Detail in that Story*. She is publisher of Chicory Blue Press.

About the Editor

Sondra Zeidenstein was born and raised in Pittsburgh, Pennsylvania. She has a B.A. from the University of Pittsburgh, M.A. from Harvard, Ph.D. from Columbia. She taught literature at Bronx Community College, Tribuvan University in Kathmandu and Dhaka University. Her poems have been published in a chapbook collection entitled *Late Afternoon Woman*. *A Detail in that Story* is her first book. She is editor of *A Wider Giving: Women Writing after a Long Silence* and two volumes of *The Crimson Edge: Older Women Writing*, and publisher of Chicory Blue Press, a small literary press that focuses primarily on writing by women past sixty-five.

Also available from Chicory Blue Press

A Wider Giving: Women Writing after a Long Silence, edited by Sondra Zeidenstein. "A masterly achievement." – May Sarton.

Heart of the Flower: Poems for the Sensuous Gardener, edited by Sondra Zeidenstein. "This is an anthology of pure delight." – Gerald Stern.

The Crimson Edge: Older Women Writing, Volume Two, edited by Sondra Zeidenstein. "*The Crimson Edge* is an inspiration, a triumph, a delight, both in human and in literary terms." – Mary Gordon.

....

Order from:

Chicory Blue Press, Inc.
795 East Street North
Goshen, CT 06756
(860) 491-2271
(860) 491-8619 fax

Please send me the following books:

_____ copies of *Family Reunion* at $18.00

_____ copies of *The Crimson Edge, Volume Two* at $17.95

_____ copies of *Heart of the Flower* at $13.95

_____ copies of *A Wider Giving* at $14.95

Name _____

Address _____

_____

Connecticut residents, please add sales tax.

Shipping: Add $4.50 for the first book and $1.50 for each additional book.